Why Do Women Write More Letters than They Send?

Why Do Women Write More Letters than They Send?

A Meditation on the Loneliness of the Sexes

DARIAN LEADER

BasicBooks
A Division of HarperCollins*Publishers*

This book was first published in Great Britain in 1996 by Faber and Faber under the title *Why Do Women Write More Letters than They Post?* It is here reprinted by arrangement with Faber and Faber.

Published by BasicBooks, A Division of HarperCollins Publishers, Inc.

FIRST U.S. EDITION

Library of Congress Cataloging-in-Publication Data

Leader, Darian.
    Why do women write more letters than they send? : a meditation
on the loneliness of the sexes / Darian Leader. — 1st ed.
        p. cm.
    Originally published: Why do women write more letters than they
post? London : Faber and Faber, 1996.
    ISBN 0-465-09169-5
    1. Women—Psychology.   2. Men—Psychology.   3. Sex differences
(Psychology)   I. Leader, Darian. Why do women write more leaders
than they post?   II. Title.
HQ1206.L387   1997
305.3—dc20   96-34933
                                                                    CIP

97 98 99 00 RRD 10 9 8 7 6 5 4 3 2 1

This book is for you, Caroline

Introduction

'I know you' is probably the worst possible thing a man can say to a woman and the best possible thing a woman can say to a man. While most men like to be included in generalizations, many women don't. This fact is well known to retailers: if you want to sell a coat to a man, you can tell him that everyone in the City or on Wall Street is wearing it, but if you want to sell it to a woman, it is better to say, on the contrary, that no one is wearing it. Hence the impossibility of writing anything about the sexes which will please, or displease, everyone.

In this book, I am trying to make a sort of collage of observations and explanations about the sexuality of men and women. What does it mean to 'be' a woman and what does it mean for her to be alone? Why might a man be impotent and to what is man and woman's jealousy really directed? A collage necessarily involves the presence of disparate elements and I hope that the particular form of unevenness which results remains suggestive. Psychoanalysts will find too much psychology, psychologists will find too little, and the reader who is neither of the above, and for whom, after all, this book is intended, will probably find much to disagree with. In contemporary gender studies, publications tend to be obscure, and accessible only to professional academics. Theorists are terrified of making mistakes and so they either do their best to conceal their real arguments or prefer to abandon argument altogether. Indeed, little research is required to demonstrate that a large percentage of male academics would rather that no one understood their conference papers than that these be subject to criticism. In this book, I have tried both to address an audience well beyond the confines of the university and to make a large number of mistakes. After all, in the early and exciting texts of psychoanalysis, curious knowledge and theory rub shoulders with ideas that today we may often find slightly ridiculous. Hence the abundance of generalizations to be found here: if many of them appear doubtful, they at least serve to invite refutation and criticism. When they are wrong, they can be replaced by other ideas and that way the ball keeps rolling. So, for example, the generalization at the start of this introduction about the shopping habits of men and women may lead to the objection that even if men want to wear what everyone else in the City is wearing and women what no one else is wearing, most men in fact end up failing to follow fashion while many women follow fashion but without necessarily wanting to. This observation raises new and challenging questions.

Readers might object that such research merely leads to socially and culturally constructed representations of sexuality, male and female. All that a book like this can do is to consolidate these stereotypes and strengthen myths about the sexes. But this sort of assumption is a veritable *source* of such myths: to argue that a psychological feature is a social construct implies precisely that there is some natural, non-socially constructed reality behind it, something more real. It is clear, however, that what is socially constructed *is* real, like an atom bomb or a hole in the ozone layer. To deny this is to underestimate the power of social and symbolic forces, which is mere fancy. The point is not that there is anything savoury or reliable in particular social constructions of sexuality, merely that their detailed study is worthwhile. If you want to modify a language, it's best to have an idea of that language first.

I have tried to pose as many questions as possible in this book about men and women. Some of them find tentative answers and others don't, but it seems to me that posing the right questions is more important than finding solutions. Thus, rather than following through one hypothesis and developing it systematically, I have chosen instead to move from one question to another. Each problem leads to other problems. The question which forms the title of this book is nonetheless given more emphasis: it serves both to open the discussion – with more questions – and to allow some of the subsequent considerations to converge. The motif which binds these together is the idea of the partner: if a letter is written but not posted, at whom or what is it really aimed? This question goes to the heart of human sexuality, which, as we shall see, is never addressed to one's flesh and blood companion, but to something beyond him or her.

These considerations also follow their own logic. Rather than focusing exclusively on clinical examples or on literature or cinema, they move from one to the other, from classical drama to romantic fiction, from the ancient pastoral to the Gothic novel, from the privacy of the consulting room to the more public space of the street or the screen. What matters here is not a treatment of any one genre but rather fidelity to *questions*: I have tried to follow such questions through regardless of cultural and chronological changes in order to make them more precise. Thus, although we might be sceptical as to the relevance of an example from the very particular milieu of Freud's Vienna, by linking it with an aspect of contemporary civilization we might see the same question being raised in a different way. The actual symptoms of some of Freud's patients may be rare today, but new symptoms have replaced them which perhaps carry similar messages.

As for the question of the title, I'm not sure that I answer it, but I hope that it will make the reader curious. A two-and-a-half-year-old boy I worked with was worried that there was a wolf at the window. A girl of the same age shared this fear. When I asked them what the wolf was going to do, the boy said that it was there to gobble him up, but the girl said 'Let's go and ask it.' As an approach to knowledge, this desire to find something out seems more reasonable, or at least more productive, than the assumption made by the little boy. This book does its best to invite the reader to share this enthusiasm for questions and to start asking them for him or herself.

In terms of orientation, this book is Lacan plus Reik: that is where many of the theoretical points and observations come from. Jacques Lacan (1901–1981) was France's most famous psychoanalytic thinker and with no doubt the most important successor of Freud. Theodor Reik (1888–1969) was one of the most industrious and canny of Freud's early students. Lacan's work has been received in the Anglo-Saxon world with great reserve. It is characterized as obscure, flighty and destined only for the initiate. This is a reputation enjoyed to such an extent perhaps only by Aristotle. Comparing the reception of the Greek thinker's work in the hundred or so years after his death with that of the Anglo-Saxon reception of Lacan so far reveals exactly the identities listed above: obscurity, flightiness, destined for the initiate. The Arabic philosopher Avicenna could say, indeed, that he couldn't understand a word of Aristotle, therefore commiting the whole of the *Metaphysics* to memory until it was explained to him many years later by a commentary of Al-Farabi. This vignette should encourage us, if not to have all of Lacan's seminars by heart, at least to offer the grace of patience. As for Reik, his reputation today is minimized by the difficulties in obtaining his books and the frequent auditory confusion of his name with that of a rather different animal, Wilhelm Reich. Not to be confused. Reik was a pupil of Freud who moved to the States after the war and published a series of urbane and insightful studies on cultural, sexual and clinical problems. He looked quite similar, in old age, to Freud and the walls of his office were covered with photographs and mementoes of his master. Despite the repetitions which frequently try the reader's sympathy, his work is that of a true researcher in psychoanalysis and is thus well worth reading today.

I have avoided heavy footnoting and quotation of authorities, a practice perhaps first made famous by Prynne, the seventeenth-century critic of the theatre teased by Milton as always having his wits beside him in the margin so as to be beside his wits in the text.

The insights and criticisms of friends and colleagues have been invaluable in the writing of this book, and I would like to thank especially Isolde Barker-Mill, Susan Bell, Marie-Laure Bromley-Davenport, Toni Marie Carlo, Madilean Coen, Véronique Gérard, Beatrice Khiara, Gretel Mitchell, Maria Olsson, Esther Palacios, William Phillips, Marie-Séverine Piard, Robert Sabel, Jennifer Scanlon, Jena Starkes and Mahan Yektai. I am indebted also for encouragement and critique to Parveen Adams, Bice Benvenuto, Malcom Bowie, Annick Bourget, Bernard Burgoyne, William Cipolla, Alison Hall, Richard Klein, Natasha Walter and Elizabeth Wright, and I have learnt much from discussions with Colette Soler and from the insights of Eric Laurent. Geneviève Morel's expositions of difficult psychoanalytic texts have been invaluable, together with her many reflections on female sexuality. The careful attention, equally friendly and critical, and the many suggestions of Julian Loose at Faber helped to shape this text from start to finish, and I have benefited continually from his advice. I hope that all the above will find much to agree and disagree with.

One

Why do men tend to keep love letters in files along with their other correspondence, whereas women often keep them with their clothes? And why do women write more letters than they post? These are questions which bring into focus some of the differences between male and female sexuality. What is involved in becoming a woman and in being a man? As we will see, neither passage is an easy one and there is nothing to guarantee the relations between the sexes, no ready formula which would tell men how to relate to women and women to men. Although a woman is often essential to a man's sexual life, we will see how the reverse is far from the case. If a woman's sexuality involves much more than the presence of a man, what else can function as her partner? To what is her sexuality directed? If we try to follow through some of these questions, perhaps it will be possible to shed some light on the problems which surround the fundamental loneliness of each sex.

This loneliness is touched when you say to your partner 'What are you thinking?' Although it has often been said that the difference between humans and animals is that animals lack the faculty of thought, the real difference is that it is only humans who habitually turn and ask each other 'What are you thinking?' Love relations frequently run aground on exactly this question. Why are 'Nothing' or 'This and that' both the best and the worst answers? Why do we find ourselves hesitating before replying and why is the question itself often felt as such an intrusion? Why do you keep asking your partner this question when you know perfectly well what the answer will be? Sexuality seems to offer a common space to join two souls, but it is more likely to be exactly what separates them. The paradox here is well known: the more you try to undo the separation, by *understanding the other person*, the more the separation is reinforced. It is not simply a question of confronting the basic difference of one's partner. Understanding wants more: it is suffocating in its very structure since it involves *asking* something. It is a demand to know something. Knowing the contents of someone else's thought turns their alterity, their otherness, into one's own property. Yet the question of whether someone else belongs to one obscures the more basic question of how much we belong to ourselves: this is something men and women fail to do in their own persistent and peculiar ways.

The psychoanalyst Jacques Lacan thought that any inquiry into the question of femininity needed to take as its point of departure the fact that 'The Woman does not exist.' This statement seems both absurd and offensive: isolated from its context, it implies a rejection of the empirical fact of the existence of females and, in addition, their lack of importance or significance in the world of men. But Lacan explained carefully the idea behind his provocative sentence: what it means immediately is that there is no univocal concept of what it is to be a woman, that there is no *essence* of womanhood. According to

Lacan, a girl may become a woman, but there is no ready made answer as to how to do this. In the psyche, there is no pre-programmed representation of the woman. In the place of feminine identity, there is a gap. No answer is automatically available as to what a woman is. Hence the key question for a girl, 'What is it to be a woman?' Is it to behave like one's mother or one's mother's friend? Is it to follow the current trend in fashion? Is it to have children? The depressions which may set in after a girl's first period are linked by some psychoanalysts to the activation of anxieties about the body or its contents. Although this may be true in many cases, the depression is also a result of the question about what a woman is: it has less to do with the surprise of the bleeding than with the surprise that in fact there is no surprise: nothing has changed. A twelve-year-old girl ran to her room to inscribe in her diary the exact time and date of her first period. The depressive effect which followed could be understood in the sense that life didn't suddenly become different: in other words, the biological change signalled in the menstruation didn't provide an answer to the question 'What is it to be a woman?' It wasn't a formula to turn one into The Woman and to start a new life. The imagined responses to the question of femininity can be multiplied indefinitely, but no one of them, biological or social, provides the ultimate solution. Lacan argued that one common response to this problem, surprising as it may sound, is to identify with a man. This is a curious thesis, that to find out what it is to be a woman, a girl will put herself in the shoes of a man. But in fact it is a perfectly logical position. Let's see why.

A man is sitting in a café and sees a couple walk past. He

finds the female attractive and watches her. Now, a woman in the same situation might well do something different. She may be attracted to the man, but will nonetheless spend more time looking at the woman who is with him. In other words, what interests her is less the man or the woman, than the *relation* between them. What does the woman have that has made this man her partner?

When Viola arrives in Illyria in Shakespeare's *Twelfth Night*, she learns that the local duke was someone known to her father and that he is in love with a certain Olivia. But rather than asking for more details about his person, as might have been appropriate given the bond between him and her father, she immediately questions of the duke's object of love, 'What's she?' The key here is that if a woman is interested in a response to the question of feminine identity, to what it means to be a woman, what better model will she have to give her a clue than another woman, one who is the object of the love or desire of a man. Viola's 'What's she?' is the feminine question *par excellence*. The first thing a woman might do on entering a man's apartment is to look for any evidence of his ex, but a man is much less likely to do this. It shows the centrality of the question of the relation of the man to another woman.

This other woman will hold the secret to the mystery of what it is that traps the desire of the man. Now, to understand a little bit more about this mystery, Shakespeare's Viola can take the place of the man in order to relate to the other woman from his position. Indeed, she disguises herself as a page and proceeds to enter the service of the duke, where she literally carries out his courtship of Olivia by proxy. It is not just dramatic convention that dictates Viola's introduction to his court in the disguise of a boy. Although so many plays of the period use the same conceit, this should not obscure the question of the significance of the gesture of disguise itself. We can note that when men dress up as women in these dramas, the result is more often than not a farce, but when women dress up as men, a veneer of seriousness is maintained. We are rarely catapulted into farce. There is something smoother, perhaps, in this gesture, indicating that the pathway of desire is not being disturbed. What it involves is, precisely, the study of someone else's desire. This would explain why so many women are interested not in one man or one woman but in couples: they will do their best to construct triangles, since a triangle is a necessary condition for the study of someone else's desire.

A series of children's games discussed by Deborah Tannen illustrates this dynamic. Playing in the kitchen area of a day-care centre, Sue decides that she wants a toy that Mary is currently guarding for herself. But rather than directly stating her desire, she tells Mary that she has come to fetch it for another little girl, Lisa, who desires it. Later, three boys are playing in the same area. When Nick sees that Kevin has the toy, he demands it for himself. Now, like Sue, Nick involves the third child, Joe, in his effort to get it, but in a very different way. Rather than appealing to the supposed desire of Joe, he simply tries to enlist Joe's help to gain possession of the object. Nick thus asserts, in a sense, his own desire, but Sue appeals to the desire of someone else. It is as if her desire depends on and is obliged to evoke the desire of the other girl. Sue claims that she is fetching the toy for someone else whereas Nick makes no such claim. Sue is saying, on one reading, that her desire is the desire of someone else. She has assumed the desire of someone else as her own.

This little scenario is exemplary of a difference between man and woman's relation to desire. The boy wants to obliterate his rival in order to win the prized object, but the girl aims less at the object than at the other girl's desire. What a woman searches for in the world around her is not an object – female collectors, after all, are extremely rare – but another desire. Hence the interest not in one man or one woman but in the relation, the desire, between them: it is no accident that women are often exceedingly interested in the romantic entanglements of their friends. Their radar is tuned to desires rather than to objects as such, and this is also perhaps the reason why women often make excellent psychotherapists or analysts: it is not that they simply evoke the figure of the mother, as some commentators have argued, but because the wavelength of desire is closer to them. That these desires are unsatisfied is a precondition: a desire satisfied is no longer a desire. The consequence here is that a woman may maintain relations with a man while always refusing to 'give' herself to him. She aims to keep the man's desire unsatisfied in order to investigate something about what such desire consists of. What is it that the man wants? What exactly does he see in her? This complicates the standard image of a woman 'playing hard to get', and shows that flirtation involves a research programme: finding out what idea of a woman a man has. Equally, running through a series of men can be a way of perpetuating the question 'What am I for him?', just as the triangle of a woman and a couple can be a way of asking 'What is *she* for him?' Both questions articulate the same fundamental inquiry into femininity.

Freud's patient Dora was the subject of his monograph *Fragment of an Analysis of a Case of Hysteria.* Treated in 1900 at the age of eighteen, she complains initially that she is being used as a pawn by her family in a complex sexual dynamic. Her father is having an affair with one Mrs K and Dora is herself the object of the seduction attempts of the husband Mr K. But as the case evolves, we find that although she protests consciously, she is in fact doing her best to maintain the structure, to make sure that the affair between her father and Mrs K continues. She is careful to leave them alone at the appropriate times and to make sure that they are undisturbed. She does this, Lacan argues in his rereading of the case, because Mrs K is in the position of someone who knows what it is to be a woman: safeguarding her father's affair with her allows Dora to maintain her questioning about what her father loves in this other woman. The father is well-suited for this latter role since he is impotent. In other words, he maintains a relation with a woman which seems to go beyond the register of coitus: what else is there that can bind a man and a woman in love? It is really the ideal triangular relation, since it involves a man loving a woman with whom he cannot copulate. She must thus have something else which makes her so attractive for the father, and this is what interests Dora. Indeed, she produces the same sort of relation with Mr K: she does not refuse to see him, but keeps him at a certain distance, thus duplicating the structure 'A man desires a woman with whom he does not sleep.' Freud kept insisting in the treatment that Dora was really in love with Mr K, but Lacan disagreed, claiming instead that love should be distinguished from identification. Dora, he argued, identified with Mr K (and with her father) to have access to the question about femininity, to approach the mystery which the figure of Mrs K incarnates. Mrs K is thus the real centre of the whole scenario. Dora has constructed a triangle and then identifies with some of the players. These identifications are discernable in her symptoms, such as coughing or throat problems. Freud's mistake here was in assuming that the husband was the Special K rather than the wife.

We see this sort of structure frequently in those women who do their best to procure partners for their friends or, indeed, their fathers. It allows them to elaborate the question of what it is in these women that the man will desire, the question of what it is to be a woman for him. The unfortunate consequence of this manoeuvre is evident. It entails that a woman will be alienated or trapped in the desire of a man, since the question 'What is it to be a woman?' is broached from the man's point of view. If this particular woman is desired by a man, what is it that he, the man, desires in her? Thus the response to the question of what a woman is becomes locked in the idea that a man is going to have of a woman. It implies also that the more one investigates the desire of these women, the more one will find out about male sexuality. Perhaps this explains why the compendiums of 'female fantasies' produced by writers like Nancy Friday often generate disbelief in their readers. Most of the scenarios seem to be invented by men, but, if we follow the above argument, there is no contradiction: the fantasies have just been 'borrowed' from men.

In Billy Wilder's film *Love in the Afternoon*, Audrey Hepburn portrays the daughter of a Parisian detective who is busy collecting evidence about the nocturnal activities of a debauched American businessman, Frank Flanagan (played by Gary Cooper). She witnesses the departure from her father's office of one of the cuckolded husbands, who intends to surprise his wife in Flanagan's hotel suite at the Ritz that night and eliminate the haggard playboy. Arriving at the Ritz just in time, she dons the veil of the guilty wife who exits via the balcony just before the husband makes his entrance. The moment of unveiling confronts the husband with his 'mistake': 'This *is* suite fourteen, you *are* Frank Flanagan . . . So you *must* be my wife,' he says to the nervous Audrey Hepburn. This is a crucial scene in that it shows us two complementary relations. First of all, that 'to be someone's wife' means simply 'to be situated in a particular place in a structure at a particular time'. It is *where* she is rather than *who* she is that counts. And second, that this *where* is precisely a *where* in relation to the desire of a man. Audrey puts herself literally into the place of another woman, a woman who is the object of a man's desire. Flanagan is renowned for his string of lovers and she tries to find a place for herself within this series. That is why the film is called *Love in the Afternoon*: the French title *Ariane* is a mistake since it focuses on her specificity, her particularity, whereas the original title indicates exactly the opposite, that love in the afternoon is simply the opposite of 'love in the morning' and 'love in the evening' with other members in a

9

series of women. Flanagan's hotel suite and ritualized ceremonial for seduction – gypsy musicians, champagne, elaborate dinner – indicate the frame within which each of his partners has to be inserted. The one moment when he meets Audrey *outside* of this frame, at the opera, he fails to recognize her. Throughout the film, she situates herself in the empty space given by the formula 'love in the afternoon', as an interchangeable element in the ceremonials of suite fourteen. Thus, she finds her being as a woman in the desire of a man, with all the alienation which this involves. She is alienated, precisely, to the formal nature of Flanagan's set of conditions: she has to be in a particular place at a particular time, the details of which are set by him, the man. When she steps outside of this framework, she is no longer desired by him.

It is only at the end of the film when Flanagan truly loves her that he finally names her 'Ariane': she is no longer one of a series of women but loved 'for what she is'. And what is this? Nothing less than a lack of being, an emptiness which never fails to reduce the cinema audience to tears: as she runs after the playboy's departing train she lists desperately all the fictional lovers she will entertain in his absence. The fabrications which she had so often elaborated to make Flanagan jealous emerge now all at once and their illusory nature becomes clear. The series of masks dissolves and we are confronted with the point of nothingness behind these images: Flanagan pulls her onto the train, kisses her and names her for the first time. The beauty of the film lies in the way in which it shows the passage from a girl – the innocent music student Audrey at the start – to a woman as a process which takes place via an alienation to the frame of a man's phantasy. To become a woman entails, in this case, giving up a part of one's being to find another form as an object of a man's desire. The obviously false backdrops of the Place Vendôme outside Flanagan's hotel window only serve to emphasize this idea of the artificial frame into which the woman is situated.

This artificiality introduces a well-known irony. If a woman so often insists on the truth, on unmasking the pretender, she is equally at home in masquerade, in ceremony and in the sort of social rituals which may appear false and artificial. It is interesting that whereas many women have as a central aim in their lives the unmasking of men, the demonstration to the man of his weakness or impotence, men keep busy by unmasking not women but *themselves*: it is no accident there are so few female clowns or that there is always a man in the pub who spends the evening by amusing others with stories of his own misfortunes. Male comedians make us laugh by pointing to their faults and weaknesses, to their castration. Thus unmasking for *both* sexes takes as its object the man, introducing another asymmetry, one which is rendered more complex by the fact that the relation to disguise is different here.

To unmask is to point to a disguise, to reveal the split between a disguise and what lies beneath it. And women, as we have just seen, are especially sensitive to this split. Policemen know very well that for male drivers they may be an intimidating representative of the law whereas for many female drivers they are simply a poor man in uniform. Hence they are either reduced, precisely, to 'poor men' or they try desperately to show their strength, often with comic effect. The traffic cop Tim Robbins in Robert Altman's film *Short Cuts* does his best to find an audience for his male prowess when he's on the job, but is incapable of convincing his family of anything beyond his own inadequacy. But what is curious is that men, in contrast to women, spend a great deal of time putting others in uniforms rather than in removing them. They like to maintain illusions about others rather than undermine these illusions. When they take off a uniform, when they focus on the gap between a disguise and what lies concealed beneath it, it is often their own disguise which is in question. Thus when a man dons a disguise himself, when he wants to be admired, when he shows his 'narcissism', he is often described as feminine. But, as Reik pointed out, what is feminine is not the desire to wear a uniform, to be admired, but rather the fact of *disguising* the desire to be admired. A female actress who is quite open about her thirst for admiration will seem much less 'feminine' than one who conceals the same wish. The relation to disguise is thus dual: on the one hand, the impulsion to unmask the man, and on the other, the respect for and the attraction towards feminine disguise, a position which indicates again the alienation to the desire of the man, the moulding of oneself to what it seems the man wants. To disguise involves finding being in this desire and to unmask shows precisely that the man is desiring, that he is incomplete, that he is lacking something . . . Wearing a disguise means to refer continuously to those who want to see you in that particular way, and removing the disguise of someone else means showing that the split, the gap, is already there in precisely this audience, that the one who watches you 'perform' is himself subject of the split between the 'performer' and whatever there is that lies behind this.

If one version of being a woman consists in conforming to the idea a man may have of woman, Wilder's film suggests an important nuance. That to put oneself in the place of another woman, as Audrey takes the place of the guilty wife at the start, is not something a woman can do on her own: or rather, if she tries to do it on her own the effect may be comic. To come to occupy this place, someone else's desire has to put her there. We see this also in the famous portrait scene in Hitchcock's *Vertigo*. The protagonist Scotty becomes obsessed with a beautiful woman who is herself obsessed, apparently, with a long dead woman named Carlotta. She goes to gaze at Carlotta's portrait in a gallery, wears the same jewellery, does her hair in the same way and so on. Now, Scotty's female friend Midge quickly becomes jealous and so she paints a portrait identical to that of Carlotta in all respects – except that in place of Carlotta's face she has painted her own. When Scotty sees this, he is furious. In a sense, he has understood that a woman for him indeed only takes on her value when she is put into the place of another woman. So Midge has understood everything perfectly except for one detail: that for a woman to move into the place of another woman, she cannot put herself there on her own. It must be another desire which gives her that place. In other words, in this context, it should have been Scotty who painted the picture. Once more, this shows the way in which a woman's 'finding a place' is so often routed through the fantasy frame of a man: to have a place means to find a place in the man's desire.

This is certainly a position adopted by many women. Confronted with the question of feminine identity, a woman may find her being in the desire of a man, conforming to the idea of a woman that she thinks the man has. But this structure is by no means universal. If the question of what it is to be a woman remains central, there is more than one way of responding to it. At the level of the unconscious, the Lady vanishes: there is no representation of her. But what is elaborated in this empty space will vary. Take the case of Agatha Christie for example. This is the story of a lady who actually vanishes empirically, yet her solution is very different from that of Dora who, contrary to Agatha, when confronted with the question of femininity, elaborated it through identification with a man.

Agatha vanishes. She vanishes just after learning of her husband's affair with another woman. The marriage has no future except, it appears, in termination. And now her empty car is found some distance from the Christie home. Her return is awaited but there is no Agatha Christie. Woods are searched, lakes are dragged but to no avail: the Lady has vanished. The public are held spellbound by the disappearance. The media run through countless scenarios to explain her whereabouts and motives and every possible refuge is investigated. But still no Agatha Christie. Until finally she is found, living tranquilly in a hotel in the North of England, playing cards, no doubt listening to talk around her about Agatha Christie's disappearance. The hotel is swamped by media and she is whisked off to London and to the consulting rooms of a psychiatrist. Now, we do not know what happened in Harley Street, but we do know what was found in the hotel register. Not the name of the authoress but another one, almost identical with that of her husband's mistress.

For more than a week she had failed to recognize herself: she had subsumed herself under the identity of another woman. The key factor here is not the imminent departure of the husband and the resultant breakup of the marriage. Rather, we could say, the husband's communication introduces, or reintroduces, the question of what it is to be a woman. What does the other woman have that makes her the object of the husband's desire? Thus the motif of 'the other woman', the incarnation of the mystery of femininity, is suddenly made present. And what does Agatha do? Rather than identifying with her husband, to find out more about this woman, she literally takes the other woman's place. It is as if a mystery story has failed to be written: Agatha herself becomes the response in her assumption of the name of the rival. The one great mystery of her life, the disappearance, is in fact precisely the failure to write a mystery story, to elaborate the possibilities around something which is not known. If this gap in knowledge is the absence of the solution to the question of what it is to be a woman, Agatha did not investigate. Rather, the answer imposed itself: to be a woman equals to be the mistress. It is a mystery story which begins with its own solution. Perhaps she found another response later in her life in her rather successful partnership with a considerably younger man: to be a woman now takes the form of being a mother.

Agatha's vanishing act evokes what is perhaps the most famous vanishing act in history: that of Helen of Troy. Whether one loves her or hates her, the daughter of Leda still represents The Woman of antiquity. The cause of so many years of war, so many wasted lives. But, curiously enough, if we follow the treatment of the story by Euripides in his *Helen*, the woman at Troy was not the real Helen. She was a phantom constructed out of the air and given to Paris by Hera in order to make sure that Paris in fact possessed nothing: meanwhile, the real Helen languishes in Egypt and dreams of the return of her husband Menelaus. This astonishing conceit recalls the motto with which we began this section, 'the Woman doesn't exist.' Helen at Troy, the most beautiful, the most loved, the most hated of women, is nothing but a mirage. The men who make claims on her are not aware that they grasp thin air: this woman who is the supreme cause of so much havoc is etherial. Euripides is showing us how the place of The Woman is, ultimately, an empty one. Behind the ideal image of Helen there is, literally, nothing. Hence it is the endeavour of each woman to find a way of making sense of this void and of constructing something in its place. If you have a hundred Chanel dresses, you can still say 'I've got nothing to wear': the one dress you don't have is the uniform of what it is to be The Woman, the definitive answer to the question of femininity. And since the place of The Woman is ultimately an empty one, there will always be a dress missing.

What about men?

Two

Being a woman is thus hardly a simple operation. In fact, the psychoanalytic argument might even seem to imply that one can only 'be' a woman in the eyes of someone else. It's always someone else who seems to be the 'real' woman, like Mrs K for Dora. Instead, it is rather a question, as we have seen, of becoming a woman, a becoming which is a continuing process rather than a single ideal point to be attained. Masculinity, of course, is also beset with problems, albeit different ones. Many recent books have tried to define the nature of these problems, yet they have had the unfortunate tendency to transform themselves into encomiums for either the 'new', weak man or the lost warrior type, something that can hardly fail to bring a smile to the reader's lips. It is a notable fact that many modest and homely gents purchase jungle warfare magazines just as furtively as the porn magazines of their adolescence. After work, in the privacy of their sitting rooms, they can learn how to survive on berries after the next nuclear holocaust and how to combat marauders with their bare hands. The popularity of these regrettable publications tells us more about the modern man than the academic volumes which treat directly of the subject.

However unfashionable it may seem today, a study of Freud's views on male sexuality can put us back on the right track, starting with the traditional emphasis on matters Oedipal. Freud deals boldly with this theme in his *Three Essays on the Psychology of Love* and starts by introducing a theoretical model supposing the existence of two original sets of impulses or 'drives': the ego drives and the sexual drives. The former are associated with the love relations with the mother and are translated in the English text as 'affectionate currents'. The latter are associated with isolated parts of the body, with erotogenic zones, the parts of the body where the child localizes pleasure. As a baby grows older, only certain zones of its body will be privileged sites of pleasure: for example, the genital area. Other areas, where the baby may have previously experienced excitement, become barren and drained of enjoyment. The key is that the ego drives aim at a person, the mother, whereas the sexual drives do not have a human being as their object: rather, they are structured around the various erotogenic zones of the body such as the mouth or the anus, the zones which have a privileged erotic value. Now, Freud argues that these sexual drives are taken up into the service of the ego drives in the same way that a small brook may be taken up into a larger river. The result is deceptive since it appears that both love and sexual currents are directed to the same object when, of course, they are fundamentally different: one is a human being, the other is a part of one's own body.

But the real problem emerges when this uneasy unification is forced to recognize that the object of the affectionate current, the mother, is now also the object of sexual desire. In other words, it knocks up against the incest barrier, the prohibition that blocks sexual relations with the mother. Now, a number of things may happen at this point: a mother substitute may be found, thus preserving the apparent assimilation of the two currents, or the two currents may split and go separate ways. The result of this first alternative is that a relation is maintained involving both love and desire directed towards the same partner, whereas in the second case the object itself becomes doubled. One woman is loved in an idealized way and another is desired sexually. The loved woman cannot be a sexual object while the sexual object incarnated in the second woman cannot be loved: hence the famous debasement of this latter figure. Brahms, for example, preserved his idealized love for Clara Schumann for so long while directing his sexual desires to prostitutes or their representatives. Goethe too, to cite another famous example, would keep, at certain points in his life, the idealized Lady at a distance while entertaining sexual relations with women of lower station whom he did not love. Often, a man will find himself sexually fettered to a woman the moment that he has finally established a love relation with someone else, showing this human necessity of doubling the object.

Freud concludes that for a relationship to be reasonably successful, the man must accept the idea of incest with mother or sister. This is a startling proposition, but it follows logically from the rest of his argument. The man's sexual problems are linked to his inability to love and desire the same person due to his refusal to confront the fact that the object of love is rather close to the mother: if he accepts this latter fact, he might be able to link the sexual currents to the amatory ones. Walpole claimed that as a child he had heard it said that a lady had asked Archbishop Tillotson for advice, for she had borne a daughter by her own son, and her son was now about to marry this daughter without knowing her identity, thus becoming her father, brother and husband. Tillotson, he says, advised the lady to leave the two to their ignorance. Perhaps behind the Archbishop's advice was the wisdom that the presence of incestuous relations is not a recipe for marital disaster, though Freud, of course, did not prescribe such unions to occur in reality. In everyday life we see this presence in a less obvious way. A man will often choose as his partner a woman who comes from a culture 'opposite' to that of the mother. And then he will try to make her behave towards him exactly as his mother treated him when he was a boy. She will stroke his hair or chide him in the same way his mother used to. The cultural distancing serves to guarantee 'This is not my mother,' so then the rest of the relationship can proceed happily, or unhappily, as if, precisely, 'This is my mother.'

Although little studied by psychoanalysis, there is a structural difference here between the incest taboo as it relates to the boy and to the girl. Most reported cases of incest involve daughter and father, uncle or elder male family member, and the frequency of reported mother–son incest is virtually zero. A girl will often experience a feeling of joy and radiance when, in her mother's absence, she goes out to a restaurant with her father and imagines that all the other diners are looking at them as if they were a couple. But when the boy goes out to dinner with his mother he doesn't have this thrill. If he does, he needs to seek professional help. The incest prohibition thus fails to generate any form of symmetry.

It is a curious fact that ancient dream interpretation

manuals include the motif of incest as a commonplace, yet today such dreams are relatively rare. Without going into the historical argument here as to why this is so, we can simply point out the paradox of such dreams when they do occur. Rather than simply confirming the received notion that beyond the figure of the partner lies the repressed image of the parent, what the incest motif also shows is that beyond the image of the parent in the dream is the problematic presence of the new love object. One of Freud's patients dreamt that he was having intercourse with both his mother and his sister: Freud remarked to him that he must have been very much in love with a girl at the time of the dream. The key here is that all the unconscious knows about women is a collection of traits drawn from the mother, for example, 'to belong to another man', 'to have a certain colour hair' and so on. When a woman is found who satisfies these criteria, there is nevertheless something more – she exists as a reality beyond the collection of preconditions, a reality for which nothing can possibly prepare the man. In the unconscious, beyond the image of the mother, the woman only exists as a gap, as a lack of representation. That is why lovers continually dwell on their first moment of sexual contact, the first kiss, the first meeting: this moment transports the lover beyond the register of preconditions (the partner must have green eyes, be linked to another man etc.) and signals the moment of the encounter with the reality of their sexuality, something for which there is no pre-programmed knowledge. Nothing will have prepared the lover for the experience. There will be something radically new in the partner and what one knows of the mother and her behaviour will not suffice to absorb or explain this.

A young man goes on a date with a woman he has met only briefly before. While they are dining in an elegant and expensive restaurant, his urbane conversation is interrupted when the lady reaches over and puts his fingers in her mouth. Yet the result is not a night with Eros but rather a two-day stay in the hospital: the man is simply not built for encounters which don't fit with the frame of his phantasy. His libido was redirected to generate unbearable stomach pains. The woman here is not included in the sexual knowledge of the man: she stepped outside his conscious and, probably, unconscious, set of rules for how a partner behaves. He simply couldn't know what she was going to do. And that is why, in running through in memory the first moments when one encountered something profoundly *new*, it is often so difficult to make the image of what happened precise, to remember the exact words or gestures. The young man spent several analytic sessions trying to describe accurately what the lady had done in the restaurant, how exactly she had taken his hand, at what moment she had closed her eyes . . . What incest dreams do is to take everything back to the parent, thus shortcircuiting, in a sense, the problem of giving a meaning and an image to the encounter with the other woman. However terrifying an incest dream might be, at least it is offering something known, even if deeply repressed, in response to the emergence of what is completely new.

The name for this frame into which the man does his best to situate his partner is phantasy. The real problem for him is whether it is possible to have any relation to a woman when its boundaries are put in question. Sharon Stone understood what was in question here in the film *Sliver*. Confronted with a disturbed young man who spends his days spying on the inhabitants of a New York tower block through closed-circuit TV, she turns her gun to blast the monitor screens and then, turning it towards him, instead of shooting, gives him the best possible advice: 'Get a life,' in other words, get a life which separates you from the (scopophilic) object of your phantasy. If all his sexual activity up until now has been put into the frame, literally, of a camera, without this support, what can he do? Sharon Stone's admonishment is no doubt the best possible advice but, as our clinical example just showed, to 'get a life' here may simply take the form of a visit to hospital. This is indeed a common result of having one's relation to the frame of one's phantasy disturbed.

Many forms of psychotherapy today do their best to re-establish this frame after some real-life experience (a meeting with Sharon Stone) has given it a knock, rather than aiming, on the contrary, to undermine it. It is the endeavour to repair the monitor screens which at least up until then had given a form of consistency to the man's life. Psychoanalysis, in contrast, tries to put this consistency in question.

Now, Freud continues to discuss the problem of doubling one's object in the case of women. His point of departure is a ritual found in many different cultures. Before a woman is to be married, she is deflowered by someone who is not her future husband. How can such a curious practice be explained? We have seen how the love life of the man was characterized by a splitting at the level of the object – the idealized Lady and the Prostitute – but when Freud turns to consider women, he suggests that this doubling is less at the level of the object than of the subject herself. This is seen in Freud's claim that the man who deflowers a woman will be the object of the two contradictory currents of love and of hate. He is loved as the husband but hated as the man who ruptures the integrity of her body. The man, in principle, is not split but the woman is the site of the splitting: she is subject to both love and hate. Her existence is characterized by the presence of these two currents. The psychoanalyst Helene Deutsch came to the same conclusion. She argued that the female version of the man's splitting his love object into two is the woman's splitting of herself, her own ego, into two: she becomes the mother and the prostitute herself. For Deutsch, this would explain the fact that a woman's daydreams may oscillate strangely between tender images of raising children and the darker worlds of the streetwalker.

But doesn't this just show us again the alienation in the desire of the man? As if she assumes the division in which the man's desire situates her: if a man splits woman into mother and prostitute, Helene Deutsch is implying that the woman, for her part, accepts and assumes this division as her own. This sort of masculine priority is present, perhaps, in the defloration ritual as well. In order for the male-oriented culture to deal with the problem, it attempts to introduce an artificial splitting before the union of wife and husband. Thus the woman must be deflowered by another man just before her wedding night:

this will hopefully channel the initial hatred away from the prospective husband. But it seems that this structure can hardly be effective. Why shouldn't the woman become bound in love to the man who deflowers her?

Perhaps it is more interesting to look at this scenario from another perspective. Note that the deflowerer does not have to be a potent man. He can be the lord of the manor, it's true, but also an old man of the tribe or even an instrument administered by an old woman. The key is in the difference, the disparity, between the future husband and this latter figure. Prior to the husband's use of his penis, a mediation is necessary, one which is situated in the symbolic register, incarnated by nothing less than a deflowerer who is, more often than not, quite the opposite of a virile figure. The deflowering ceremony is a rite in the strict sense of the word – something which is symbolic. It shows that the penis is distinct from the phallus, which is purely symbolic, and that is why the introduction of a real organ is not necessary: an instrument will suffice. What matters is the distinction between the two registers, incarnated by the real figure of the husband and the symbolic properties of the deflowering agent.

The indigenous cultures which Freud refers to here present another clear articulation of this distinction. Anthropologists and psychoanalytic commentators in the early part of this century had been puzzled by the fact that a woman's pregnancy is often attributed, in such cultures, to an encounter with a spirit of some sort rather than to coitus with the husband. She is pregnant not because of the man's penis but because she walked past a certain brook or cluster of rocks. Many commentators used this belief as material to support racist notions of the undeveloped mentality of 'natives'. How, they argued, could these people be so blind as not to see that there is a causal link between coitus and pregnancy? But in fact, what the indigenous belief shows is an authentic understanding of the difference between the real penis and the symbolic dimension: as in the ritual of deflowering, we see that the husband's penis is not enough. Something else must mediate the relation between the sexes. The symbolic side of this element is obvious: a spirit who dwells in a brook or group of rocks cannot be seen or touched. It is not a question of something tangible. This contrasts, of course, with the baser tangibility of the male organ.

The importance of a symbolic mediation is illustrated in Longus' short novel *Daphnis and Chloe*. This tells the story of a young boy and a young girl on a pleasant Greek island. Everything is fine except for the fact that they spend the whole of the book trying to go to bed together and fail systematically. It is like a classical version of Freud's *Three Essays on the Theory of Sexuality*, that is, a list of all the things that can go wrong with the sexual relation. They try copying the animals but this proves fruitless: something blocks the transition from the natural world to the world of human desire. Finally, they are able to make love but only thanks to one crucial condition: the arrival of Daphnis' master, a man who up until then had been 'merely a name', in other words, someone who incarnates the symbolic dimension. With his sanction and his implicit gaze on their lovemaking, the form of mediation is provided which shows that there is no continuous passage from nature (copying the animals) to culture (making love). Rather, there is a profound discontinuity. The same mediation was necessary for Kim Basinger and Alec Baldwin: it is no accident that the tempestuous nature of this association of bank robbers in the most recent film version of Jim Thomson's novel *The Getaway* is tempered only at the close of the film by the blessing of an old man who has little to do with the preceding narrative. As they escape to freedom across the Mexican border in his truck, he gives them a little commentary on their union in the classical religious sense: the relation between a man and a woman is mediated by the speech of an elder, exactly as it is at a marriage ceremony. In the book, there isn't this mediation, and the couple seem more interested in tearing each other apart.

This emphasis on the symbolic dimension is shown with increasing clarity in the popular cinema, focusing most often on the problem of masculinity. We are shown time and again that to be a man requires more than to have the biological body of a male: something else must be added to it. In the science fantasy *Innerspace*, a wimp is turned into a real man by having a miniature submarine injected into his bloodstream. The pilot of the submarine is by no means a wimp and the tension between pilot and host organism provides much of the film's humour. But what matters here is less the fact that the sub is piloted by an authentic 'hero' than that something symbolic, a production of science, has been incorporated by the body. To be a man means to have a body plus something symbolic, something which is not ultimately human. Hence the frequent motif of the man machine, from the *Six Million Dollar Man* to the *Terminator* or *Robocop*. It is worth noting that in the film about the latter the hero is recognized by the particular trait of spinning his gun before holstering it. The Robocop is a family man who is destroyed by thugs, then rebuilt as a robot by science. His son always insists, before the transformation, that his human father perform the gun spinning trick he sees on TV. When the robot can finally do this properly, he is no longer just a male biological body: he is a body plus machinery, a body which includes within it the symbolic circuitry of science. Old heroes had bits of metal *outside* them (knights), but modern heroes have bits of metal *inside* them. To be a man today thus involves this kind of real incorporation of symbolic properties.

A contrast emerges here with earlier forms of civilization, characterized by the manifest presence of initiation rituals. The son must go through an ordeal, or at least a ceremony, in order to take on his place as a man in society. These tasks are specified and often finely orchestrated. But today, what remains, in our culture, of the initiation ceremony, of the formalized passage to adulthood? What we see in its place are mad forms of initiation, as if the initiation ceremony takes place not in a symbolic, ritualized framework, but literally in the real. Witness the recent case of the two teenagers who carried out a brutal and contingent murder to join the ranks of the SAS, the real men forever on the horizon. The less a civilization provides a symbolic framework for initiation, the more it will return in a crazy, real form. It shows the need of symbolic form for masculinity to be assumed: there must always be something more than the biology.

The paradox, as Lacan pointed out, is that the more 'masculine' the behaviour of a man becomes, the more he is transported into the feminine, the dimension of parade or, to use an old-fashioned term, seeming. The more a man today tries to behave like a real man, the more false and affected his actions appear. It is no accident that the Hollywood star chosen for the role of the world's first pregnant man was Arnold Schwarzenegger. This man is more of a man than his colleagues: he wrestles with monsters, battles with liquid metal killers, eliminates villains and ruffians of all denominations. He has muscles in places where other stars don't even have places. And now he becomes, in the film *Junior*, literally feminized. But in a sense, this fate was the only logical turn to his career: the more the attributes of manliness are exaggerated, the more feminine the result. The crucial detail is that these attributes are not transmitted symbolically here: they have to be sought 'outside'. It is the body itself which has to be transformed, precisely because there is a problem in the symbolic transmission. Schwarzenegger is the ultimate self-made man in this sense: his body itself has been built up, making of him both a symbol and a camp caricature of capitalism. If the attributes of manliness are not passed on in symbolic ways, men try to grasp them 'from the outside' and the symbolic structure has to be literally injected, be it in the form of the submarine of *Innerspace* or the circuitry of the Robocop.

The cultural formations we have just discussed show the importance of a dimension in sexuality which is not strictly speaking human. It is symbolic, alien to the biological reality of the organism. When the sexes meet, there must be some form of symbolic mediation. There is never just 'a man' and 'a woman', but rather, 'a man', 'a woman' and 'a spirit', for example. One might argue here that the deflowering ritual discussed by Freud involves in fact something much simpler than all this nonsense about symbolic dimensions. Is it not simply a way of ensuring fertility for the marriage that will follow? It is erroneous, however, to identify the phallus and the idea of fecundity. The phallus is not the organ or the symbol of fertility but the symbol of a register beyond the real side of the copulation. We can see this in the use of the phallus in classical cultures: rather than being placed in the bedroom or in the fields to promote fertility, they are found at crossroads and limit points, marking boundaries. It is thus linked less to growth and plenty than to symbolic limits. As the classical scholar Walter Burkert points out, if the idea was merely to symbolize union, why do we not find classical stone phalli pointing into the earth: instead, we find them pointing upwards, hardly an appropriate way of promoting fertility in the land. The use of the phallus in the deflowering rituals would thus indicate the dimension of a symbolic framework, necessary to sanction the ensuing real sexual activity between husband and wife.

So far, everything seems to point to the sexual motives of the man, the future husband, in the scenario. He aims to avoid the bride's possible hostility towards him and to register his own sexual organ beneath the symbol of the phallus. But Freud offers us a number of further suggestions as to the rite. We saw how the problematic of male sexuality was treated from the perspective of the collision of sexuality and the incest barrier. When the affectionate and the sexual drives knock up against this prohibition, they split to produce the idealized lady and the debased one. But in the case of a woman, Freud argues, it is less a question of the clash between sexuality and the incest barrier than the fact that the sexuality is constructed out of the incest barrier itself. Sexuality does not collide with prohibition, it is based on it. Freud's example is the observation that young girls frequently keep their first love relations secret from their parents, however liberal and relaxed they might in fact be. The relation must be kept at the level of the secret: in other words, the girl imposes a barrier on her sexual life and its expression. Even if the structure of the family is rather different today than it was in early twentieth-century Vienna, it is still a fact that girls so often make and maintain friendships by the telling of secrets.

If we accept Freud's argument so far, this observation will refute a popular misconception about lovemaking. We often hear of the male fantasy of making love in public places, but the fusion of sexuality and secrecy implies, on the contrary, that such scenarios will be closer to feminine versions of sexuality. The idea of coitus in a space which is public, close to the gaze of others and yet simultaneously hidden from them, would be an empirical example of constructing sexuality from prohibition: the space of the secret and the sexual space are one and the same.

Now, if a woman requires something forbidden or secret about a love relation, what will happen when she marries and the relation becomes legitimized in a formal way? The argument suggests that she will gravitate to another relation outside the marriage to maintain the condition of forbiddenness. In Freud's conception there is hardly even the possibility of a harmonious relation between a man and a woman. The man will be attracted to two women (at least), and the woman to a relation outside the marital or established one. It is not simply a question of one partner and their mate. There is a fundamental division at the level of the relation between the sexes.

But surely not all of this squares with experience. A woman may in fact find it easier to remain faithful to her partner than a man does. A survey on male and female fidelities is interesting here. Asked if they would prefer their partner to make love with someone else and think about them, or make love with them and think about someone else, the majority of women questioned say that they would prefer their partner to sleep with another woman while thinking of them. The men, on the contrary, say that they would prefer their partner to sleep with them while thinking of another man. The obvious interpretation of this material would be to say that men are more possessive, but surely this misses the point: the women are equally possessive, but their possessiveness has a different object, the man's love rather than, as with the man, their body. Perhaps what this shows is that men understand that women are always aiming at another man who is beyond them anyway, and, furthermore, that this man is not a real, flesh and blood one. He is more likely to be a ghost, which means that a woman may remain physically faithful to a man while at the same time she deceives him: as she takes him into her arms, she may be embracing a phantom which is beyond him.

Psychoanalysts Eric Laurent and Geneviève Morel have both pointed out the interest of the recent film version of

Dracula for a study of female sexuality. The heroine's choice is between Keanu Reeves and the living dead, and she chooses the living dead. Given the popularity of Keanu Reeves, this seems a surprising choice. But it shows, nonetheless, the way a woman's partner may be something more important than a real life, flesh and blood man, one who has a reflection in a mirror. This is perhaps one of the reasons for the remarkable and unexpected success of the film *Truly, Madly, Deeply*, in which a woman mourns her deceased lover to such an extent that he literally returns to live with her. After the first ecstatic day with him, things start to go wrong for the simple reason that now, precisely, he isn't enough of a ghost. He's there in person with all his noisy friends, messing up the house, watching videos, getting in the way. In other words, doing all the things that a real man does. When she finally establishes her relation with another, flesh and blood man, he can become a ghost once again and constitute the object of her longing. This splitting between the real man and the ghost, we can conjecture, is what will make the relation with the new boyfriend liveable. When the ghost became 'real', there was no longer the possibility of the bifurcation between the real and the ghostly.

A woman came to see me with the unlikely idea that psychoanalysis would make her lover's behaviour less erratic. She complained of the unexplained disappearances which followed each of his visits to her apartment. But it soon became clear that these disturbances were in fact essential to the relation which unconsciously she wished to maintain. Describing the scenario as if it were entirely new, it turned out after some questioning that this had been going on for some ten years. And that, furthermore, a most peculiar ritual had been established. Each time the man left, she would telephone all the morgues in the town in which she lived, giving a description of the man and asking if a body had been found. After all these years, she knew the phone numbers by heart and the morgue employees would recognize her voice immediately. Does this not suggest that beyond the figure of her lover was the shadow of a dead man? Beyond the living lover who would spend time with her was the corpse she searched for. In contrast to the lady of *Dracula*, instead of finding two figures to incarnate the live man and the dead one, she managed to focus them on a single man. This search for a dead man as lover is perhaps the reason why people are so often amazed at the fact that a friend has fallen in love with the most incredibly boring man. Men who are particularly boring shouldn't worry too much about finding a partner, since it is perhaps precisely for their mortification that they will be loved. Beyond the register of the living is the love a woman claims from the dead man.

This phantom who claims his bride is likely to be associated with the man who can separate a daughter from her mother. In fairy tales, knights don't just 'find' princesses, they find them in the clutches of wicked witches, and then they rescue them. There is frequently an erotic effect linked to this sort of rescuer, and we can see this in the way in which a man may suddenly lose all sexual attraction for a woman from the moment that he shows some sort of complicity with her mother. He is no longer the wedge to separate them. Men sometimes complain about the enigma of this operation: they are just trying to be nice to the mother, they say, because they love the daughter so much. But this means paying a price in terms of their own erotic value. It is much more sensible for a man who wants a woman to like him more to be nice not to her mother but to cats. Many women not only like cats but like men who like cats.

Freud's notion of the condition of forbiddenness becomes even more startling when he tells us that it represents the female equivalent of the male tendency towards debasement of the object. This is a remarkable claim. Debasement for the man involves the image of unadulterated sexual pleasure with a woman who is not greatly valued, the image of a sort of pure lust or pleasure. But if the female equivalent of this is the condition of forbiddenness, it would imply that the female version of pure sexual pleasure is, more or less, a lack of pleasure, sexuality with the prohibition. Thus one might be tempted to infer that woman's sexuality would involve a kind of lack of sexuality, a sort of implicit subtraction.

One hasty way to understand this peculiar idea would be to evoke the theme of frigidity. Just as Freud had concluded that most men are impotent, in the sense that they fail to combine the two currents of sex and love, one might conclude that many women are frigid. This interpretation is not acceptable. Although there is a very real asymmetry between male impotence and female frigidity – it is not infrequent for a man to consult an analyst for a problem of impotence yet it is almost unheard of for a woman to consult an analyst complaining of frigidity – the key to the problem does not lie with this proposition. To understand something about the barriers which a woman might have to engage with, male potency problems need to be distinguished. We are in a register different from the male complaint of the Italian physician Cardano: 'Not servitude to my father, not poverty, not illnesses, not enmities, quarrels, injuries from citizens, rejection by the medical profession, false calumnies, and that infantile heap of troubles could drive me to despair, hatred of life, contempt of pleasures and perpetual sadness: this one thing certainly could.' Impotence is unbearable for this subject as for many men.

The Viennese psychoanalyst Edmund Bergler found it curious that a morning erection is never counted as a true, sexual one. It is associated in general with an unemptied bladder. But this supposition must be false, since if it were not, the cure for impotence would be simple: a man could refrain from urinating for several hours before intercourse. The explanations and rationalized excuses for impotence are multiple. And even the most sophisticated tend to consist of mere fancies served up with the condiment of science. The classical psychoanalytic idea which appeals to the notion of *vagina dentata* is clearly mistaken. It supposes that a man will be reticent to insert his penis into the vagina due to an unconscious fantasy of the woman's sex having teeth which might bite off his organ. But surely this is refuted by the empirical observation that men suffering from problems of potency prefer to be given fellatio, which involves the introduction of the penis into the one part of the woman's body that really does have teeth.

A better explanation would evoke the notion of the symbolic phallus that we discussed earlier in the context of defloration rituals. We saw how the man's use of the real penis had to be sanctioned by a certain symbolic framework: there will always be something beyond the organ itself. In cases of impotence, the man often has the fantasy that his partner has slept with many other men first. Thus we could say that the problem is not in the fear of an encounter with the vagina's teeth but rather with the phallus of the other man. For a man to be potent, there must be an implicit acceptance that there will always be something beyond his own penis, probably to be identified as the phallus of the father (although not necessarily the real father). We saw this in our discussion of the ritual of deflowering and the belief in the spirit's participation in pregnancy: there will always be something beyond the man's real organ. This phallus, forever out of the subject's reach, will necessarily make the real penis smaller. This would explain why apparently even the most well-endowed men can worry about the size of their organ, and the fact that there exist men who, in a public convenience, are unable to urinate if another man is standing next to them. The value of the penis is directly affected by the shadow of the other man. If the male subject does not resolve this necessary incommensurability in the appropriate way, there may well be a problem of potency. This thesis may be tested: if a woman makes a reference to a past lover, or better, to the phallic prowess of a past lover, just before intercourse, it is more than likely that her partner will become impotent. A well-timed reference to the fact that her last boyfriend had the body of a Greek god may be all that's necessary . . . It is certain that if any of Penelope's 108 suitors had spent a night in her arms, they would have been impotent, since beyond her is the phallus of the man they are not, Odysseus. Hence the problem of potency and the necessity of interpreting Cardano's reference to the 'servitude of my father' in a sense rather different from the one he intended.

Such potency problems may occur if the man's relation with the father remains unresolved on the level of an imaginary battle: if there is a failure to register the symbolic difference between father and son in the right way. In such cases, the subject is a bit unhappy that there is a phallus beyond his own. Like Lord Byron, he may attempt to steal women from his father rather than to structure his relations with women beneath a paternal, symbolic sanction. If the Oedipal complex operates smoothly, the son will receive the phallus from his father, but strictly for later use: it is something for the boy's future. The American version of the complex would be: 'Some day son, all this will be yours . . .' Perhaps this is why men tend to get excited about changing the planet, about creating new visions of the future, whereas women often seem more concerned with *preserving* the planet, with restoring it to what it used to be. It's the difference between the phallic version of the future and a concern for the past.

If the central problems of male impotence revolve around the relation to the phallus, things are rather different for a woman. Let us first point out that the concept of frigidity is a suspect one. Analysts have never really agreed on what it might mean. To define it as the absence of vaginal orgasm would be a bit silly: whereas Bergler had the idea that a woman is frigid if she fails to experience involuntary muscular contractions around the vagina during each intercourse, Helene Deutsch eventually arrived at the peculiar conclusion that not only is vaginal orgasm most unusual but that the vagina isn't a sexual organ at all. A prudent inquiry would have to redefine its object here as a plural, as *frigidities*, as the term does not denote any one single state. And likewise, an individual might believe that a particular state of the body counts as frigidity when their neighbour would hardly have the same idea. Bergler describes a spectacular example of this sort of parallax in the field of male sexuality. A man complains of premature ejaculation, but Bergler finds out that in fact the man can perform coitus for around half an hour before releasing his seed: he had been convinced that any ejaculation was premature if it preceded the orgasm of his partner. He had clearly failed to understand the most basic fact about sex: that intercourse ends at a different time for a man and a woman. It is also well known how a whole generation of women in the States were told by sexologists that they were 'frigid' if they didn't have a vaginal orgasm, defined in the most arbitrary way by the experts. When Lacan discusses the problem of frigidity in 1958 it is not from the perspective of the orgasm but rather from that of the 'sensitivity to enclosing the penis', something very different. If we want to elaborate on the Freudian thesis we deduced from reading *The Taboo of Virginity*, we need to follow a different path. To do so, let us turn to the problem of masturbation.

It is remarkable how contemporary studies in the psychoanalysis of women ignore this question. Whereas the early post-Freudians often wrote on this theme – the briefest survey of the minutes of the Vienna Psychoanalytic Society shows that for years they chattered about little else – it is hardly ever discussed today in published work in the psychoanalytic world. And yet it would be absurd to deny the place it occupies in the sexual lives of many women. This is a place far removed from the one it holds for a man, where it is frequently linked to the Oedipus complex and the guilt associated with this. Women perhaps feel less guilty masturbating, whereas men often complain of exactly this sentiment. When men masturbate, their activity is generally combined with a fantasy scenario, an image of intercourse of some sort with a woman. It is an image of sexual pleasure, one perhaps more on the side of the debased woman of Freud's schema than that of the idealized lady. Now, things are rather different for a woman. There exist many anthologies of women's sexual fantasies, the problems of which we have touched on earlier. One has to be especially wary of the so-called 'data' here. Let's focus on one woman's fantasy included in an analytic study of masturbation carried out in the 1940s. Although this might seem out of date, the example allows us to focus on issues which emerge repeatedly in clinical practice today. The men in the survey tend to privilege images of lust and of sexual pleasure but the one woman whose case is discussed has the following image: she asks her husband to have intercourse with her. He refuses and leaves her for another woman.

This is a curious scenario. Rather than focusing on an image of sex, it is apparently based on the image of a lack of sex. The place of the woman is one of vanishing, of sub-traction from the sexual scene. The other parties will have sex, it seems, not her. This is in striking contrast to male sexuality. The woman here seems to link an erotic value to her own subtraction, to privilege it, in a sense, whereas men will do everything precisely to avoid their own disappearing. What this means, for a man, is that he will desire a sexual relation with a woman but will do everything he can to remain in control. Since an encounter with a woman's sexuality may well have the opposite effect, he may opt to put another man, perhaps his best friend, in his place. We see this, for example, with the poet Shelley. Each time he establishes a relation with a woman, he attempts to abdicate his place to a friend, Jeff Hogg: for his first wife Harriet, and Mary, and even his sister. He repeatedly tries to engineer a union between this privileged male friend and the woman he loves or desires.

Lacan discusses this structure in his article 'Direction of the Treatment'. A patient comes up with the idea that his mistress should sleep with another man and that he should watch. This is a relatively frequent male fantasy scenario. We see it in our experience in the relations of many men with their best friends. An antique version may be found in Herodotus, where we learn how King Candaules proposes to hide his bodyguard Gyges in his room so that he can see his wife naked. This is what Lacan refers to earlier in his collection of papers on psychoanalysis, the *Ecrits*, where he speaks about 'abdicating one's desire'. The subject places the phallus on the side of the imaginary other, the friend, and the enjoyment he is deprived of is passed over to the counterpart.

Lacan said that in this respect men are like frogs. They puff themselves up in situations of danger and don't want anyone to see their real condition. The idea is that the phallic nature of the subject's position in his fantasy is so accentuated that any passage to the level of sexual action will fail: he therefore dreads precisely what he aspires to, since it would confront him with his deflation. Hence the appeal to the counterpart to act in one's place and Lacan's formulation that the obsessional maintains his desire as forbidden. It's the sort of action by proxy that we find in Goldsmith's aptly titled play *The Good-Natured Man* where the sweet and kindly Mr Honeywood carries out a courtship in the place of his friend Mr Lofty even though he loves the girl himself. Whereas the psychoanalyst and Freud biographer Ernest Jones had argued that the subject fears *aphanisis*, the complete extinction of his desire, Lacan's formulation here implies the contrary: rather than fearing *aphanisis*, he takes refuge in it. Rather than entering the arena of his desire, the obsessional is always, and with reason, somewhere else. He will have another man act for him and take his place, with the obvious consequence of a feeling of alienation or even mortification.

This corpse-like quality of many obsessional men attracted the attention of Lacan, who gave a formula for their central preoccupation: 'Am I alive or dead?' What seems to be an abstract question is in fact a very real problem for these men. They can be 'dead' in the sense that they live via someone else, as our examples have just shown, or 'dead' in the sense of mortified by routine, pattern or verbal impositions. Some men have to comment on or explain, to the irritation of those around them, every action. Instead of going to get a cup of tea, they go to get a cup of tea *and* say 'I'm going to get a cup of tea'. Or, they organize their day according to a hopelessly precise timetable, writing lists and making sure that everything is in its place. Their routine literally mortifies their lives. This is also why hysterics are so often attracted to obsessional men: obsessionals do their best to represent corpses and hysterics do their best to make corpses come alive. A hysteric is someone to whom things are always happening, whereas an obsessional is a thing to whom people are sometimes happening (people in the sense of the living, what isn't dead). While the man tries to read the newspaper at the appointed time, the woman tries to disrupt his routine, to talk or to do something else, to get rid of the tyranny of the newspaper. And the woman is closer to the truth here, since the man, in mortifying his life, is trying to forget the fact that he is alive, when, of course, he is. Hence the common hysterical admonishment to the obsessional man, 'Stop being so boring' (or, at a party, 'Dance!'), which can be translated as 'Show me that you're not dead.' Thus, however difficult their unions may be, hysterics and obsessionals are really quite well-suited to each other.

This mortification is no doubt the reason for Antonio's famous sadness at the start of *The Merchant of Venice*. Scholars have continually debated the cause of the mysterious and unexplained malaise which opens the play. Antonio's 'I know not why I am so sad' is as enigmatic as the subsequent riddle of the three caskets, but rather than following those commentators who attribute the sadness to an unconscious homosexual attraction to his friend Bassanio, why not see it as the result of just the sort of structure we have been discussing? Antonio lends a great deal of money to his friend so that he can pursue the lady Portia with due ceremony and style, yet he seems to have no love object himself. One puts one's best friend into one's own place: Antonio is not attracted to Bassanio, but rather, in a sense, he *is* Bassanio. The debt he contracted to help Bassanio was not repaid in time and he was obliged to forfeit a pound of flesh: much of the play's action concerns his escape from this grim condition. It is remarkable, but no doubt perfectly logical, that at the end of the play he makes himself the stake of yet another foolhardy wager, staking his very soul on the success of Bassanio and Portia's marriage, when in fact many clues in the text indicate that this success is far from certain. He is fatally trapped in the triangle of desire but is always somewhere else – in the place of his friend. He gives up any sexual enjoyment of his own and passes it over to his imaginary counterpart, Bassanio.

It is amusing to note that this concept of *aphanisis*, of the disappearance of pleasure, was introduced by Jones. This meticulous man was himself the subject of a series of inexplicable disappearances: Freud questioned one of his colleagues during a psychoanalytic congress held in an Austrian hotel as to the whereabouts of the Welsh analyst. Apparently, he would slip away without telling anyone where he was off to. It might be tempting to project a novel or a play with the title *The Disappearance of Ernest Jones,* thus giving his absences the dignity of those of Agatha Christie. However, a glance at his biography makes certain explanations more probable than others: like Bertrand Russell, this thinker was hopelessly infatuated with women on a regular basis, more likely to be with one of the female employees of the hotel than a distinguished analytic colleague.

Now, let's return for a moment to Lacan's patient who proposes to his mistress that she sleep with another man. His mistress replies to this plan to save his failing potency with a dream which she proceeds to relate to him. She dreams that she has a phallus as well as a woman's sex, but that she nonetheless desires the phallus. Now, the dream does not simply indicate, as one might suppose, that the mistress desires to be a man and a woman. We may remember that Helene Deutsch had a similar dream during her analysis with Freud and she could never accept his interpretation that she wanted to be both boy and girl. It was only later, when she heard the psychoanalyst Karl Abraham lecturing on the castration complex, that she understood why Freud's explanation had seemed incomplete. In other words, a dream like this involves a reference to *castration,* the fact that having a phallus does not stop one from desiring one. There is a difference between the image of the penis – something the body can have or not have – and the symbol of the phallus, which serves to symbolize desire and the human dimension of lack. It is a symbol of desire, of what we never reach and of what we have to give up to become men and women. We experience this lack whenever we travel on the London Underground with a one-way ticket: there is always a peculiar sensation when the machine at the station exit does not return our ticket. Even if we know that the machine will retain it, there is a split-second shock that we don't have it, that something is not returned to us. That is what castration is, the fact of giving up something for nothing. Most people who cheat on the Underground do so because of their unresolved relation to castration: either because they want something in return for what they have given up, or because they want to continually experience the castration, represented now by the encounter with the inspector. Castration is thus not a real operation on an organ but a symbolic dimension of human existence.

The dream of the mistress of Lacan's patient involves this symbolic dimension and not simply the imaginary nature of the 'wish to be a boy and a girl', indeed, exactly the sort of wish that the patient used as an alibi: he said to Lacan that he thought he was homosexual. The phallus that Lacan's patient situated on the side of the other man is an imaginary one: there is still the dimension of desire and its reference, the symbolic phallus, one which is impossible to restitute to the imaginary body. This non-coincidence of the imaginary and the symbolic phallus is seen in the old Egyptian myth of Isis and Osiris. Isis searches for the scattered remains of her murdered brother Osiris, retrieving all of them apart from the penis. So in its place she erects phallic monuments to commemorate the lost organ, showing how the phallus comes into the place of the lack of the penis. The scattered remains of the body are thus distinguished from the phallic signifier. The dream of the mistress of Lacan's patient shows clearly the impossibility of this restitution. The phallus as a signifier is distinct, as the dream shows, from the question of having or not having the penis. There is thus a change in the value of the phallus for the subject here: it is less the imaginary object which he seeks via the other man than a signifier of desire.

Men, then, do their best to avoid disappearing. Hence they may well have the fantasy of watching their partner sleep with another man. But one might object here, why is it then that a man masturbates with the image of himself having intercourse with a woman? It would seem more logical to have the image of the other party. The answer is a very simple one: to masturbate with an image in one's head means not having to confront the woman in a real sexual encounter. It is the latter that will make him disappear and hence the relative security of a sexual relation not with a woman but with one's own body. This is what will allow the man to focus on an image of 'pure jouissance'. ('Jouissance' means too much excitation, felt as pleasure or pain.) But the woman's relation to masturbation is different here. Her fantasy is of asking her husband for intercourse, his refusing and leaving her for another woman. There is no manifest representation of what we might call sexual pleasure. But the key is not the fantasy *per se*, but the fact that she masturbates to it. In other words, the fact that her sexual pleasure, the jouissance of her body, is linked to the image of subtraction, of the lack, in a certain sense, of sexual pleasure. We could call this structure *the sexualization of her own disappearance.*

This should by no means be confused with the supposed masochism which early analysts often ascribed to women. Sandor Rado, for example, had the idea that when a girl becomes aware of her lack of a male sexual organ, the pain of privation becomes sexualized to produce a new pleasure, 'a new gratification' which is ultimately masochistic because it is generated in a comparison with what boys apparently 'have'. The sexualization we are discussing here is different: as we will see, it is not a pleasure based on the idea that someone else has something better.

A contrast between male and female fantasy scenarios in the field of jealousy can make things more precise. When a man is confronted with the infidelity of his lover, he may well entertain the idea of murdering his female partner or, less commonly, his male rival. But despite feelings of rage and revenge, a woman is often likely to wish for her own disappearance rather than that of one of the other parties. The response to the question of the fidelity of the man's love takes the form of her own subtraction, her death. When Helena is confronted with the withdrawal of Bertram's love in *All's Well that Ends Well*, her first thought is to disappear. This shows how closely linked love and existence are for a woman. Sometimes, indeed, the experience of the loss of the partner's love will produce the almost uncanny feeling for a woman of being a stranger to herself. She might even change her appearance quite radically (the colour of her hair, her clothes, etc.).If another person's love may supply her with a measure of being, its withdrawal may entail literally becoming another person – as was the case, perhaps, for Agatha Christie.

The problem is that the purity of a love that a woman demands will not find an empirical man to incarnate it: that is why some women choose to assure themselves of the one love that is guaranteed, the love of God, and why, in general, the man that a woman aims at is never a real man. Real human beings don't love continuously: their sentiments oscillate between love, hate and indifference. A woman unsure of the fidelity of man's love says 'I just *know* God loves me. I've always known it, but I can't explain why.' To find a continuous love, a love that won't let you down, one has to go beyond the human register, perhaps, indeed, to the register of the dead man. After all, with real live human love, the only logical thing that can happen is that it ends.

To be rejected by the male partner will often trigger a renewed questioning of what one is, what value one has, whereas for a man the stakes are somewhat different. Such a reaction in a man would be indicative of a neurosis. It is rare for a man to wonder about 'what he is' after a rejection in love. One could contrast the man's behaviour with the way in which a disappointed woman will renew links with her mother. The man is more likely to turn to a so-called mother substitute. What does this show? Perhaps that, for a woman, beyond the figure of every male partner, however much such a man may resemble the father, there is the figure of the mother. This is the conclusion that Freud came to in his work on femininity. If we take this argument seriously, it would explain why so many love affairs run aground. Beyond the ideal of the father that a woman may seek in her partner, there will be the original tempestuous relation with the mother.

The classical explanation is that we fall out of love when we become aware of the gap between our ideal of the partner and the real person we have a relationship with. The failure of love is thus seen as a realization of the distance between the real and the ideal. Thus Bertrand Russell, for example, could explain the exhaustion of his love for his first wife with the phrase 'she was no longer the saint I had always supposed her to be'. But if we follow our logic, the problem is not in the distance between real and ideal, a problem which, after all, is confronted by all lovers. Everyone eventually wakes up and realizes that they've been dreaming a little bit. The real problem would lie, on the contrary, in the gap between two contradictory ideals: the ideal of the father and the ideal of the mother, if we accept the thesis that beyond the appeal to the father is the dark shadow of the relation with the mother. The traits represented by the father will never be identical with those represented by the mother: weakness and strength, for example. It is thus less a question of the inadequacy of the real partner to live up to the ideal than the fact that what one aims at, at the level of the ideal, is basically an impossibility, the coalescence of two contradictory sets of traits.

In Russell's case – although, as we have seen, he rationalized his break with his first wife in terms of a realization of the gap between the real and the ideal – surely it is significant that he tells us that he fell out of love with her on the same page of his three-volume autobiography that he describes his discovery of the famous 'Russell paradox'. This logical problem involves nothing less than the contradictory presence of two different ideals: the existence of sets which are members of themselves and the existence of sets which are not. The set of all spoons is not itself a spoon but the set of all abstract objects is an abstract object. The tension between these two conditions, together with the assumption that all properties (to be a spoon, to be an abstract object . . .) determine sets, generates the paradox. Without going into the details of the logic here, we can note that not only does Russell choose to tell us about these events on the same page, but he consistently uses the vocabulary of the lover in his descriptions of the paradox: its discovery, he writes, 'put an end to the logical honeymoon that I had been enjoying'. Likewise, his first encounter with Euclidean geometry was 'as dazzling as first love'. These clues suggest that there is a link between the discovery in logic and the relation with his wife, one which revolves around the inconsistent presence of ideal properties. And don't we feel so often that our partner wants two different, incompatible and contradictory things from us?

A further contrast is of interest here. When a man is confronted with the infidelity of a partner, he is likely to be tortured by images of sexual intercourse between his rival and his mate. But when a woman entertains such images they are much more likely to focus on scenes of affection between the two parties, an intimate conversation, words spoken in bed and so forth. Details of what the other woman looks like will also be much more important for her than the details of a male rival may be for the man. If a woman tells her partner of her infidelity, the man is more likely to ask of his rival 'What does he do?' than 'What does he look like?' The image of sex for a woman is relatively rare. In other words, what matters for her are the relations of love between the male partner and the other woman. Now, why should speech be so important here? Why are love relations so often imagined as a pact of speech while the sex seems to be relegated to a secondary place?

Women are certainly wooed with words. Reik discussed the way in which Desdemona falls in love with Othello as he is *telling* her of his adventures, choosing him instead of the younger, more handsome suitors surrounding her at the time. His speech is the crucial factor. It is curious how women are often captivated by a man's speech even when they know perfectly well that he is deceiving them or engaged in a deliberate seduction ploy. The power of the word remains basically the same. Doris Day didn't sing, 'I want to be dated': she sang 'I want to be dated and narrated'. We see this also in the way in which women often wish the man to speak to them while they are making love together. A woman could only achieve real sexual satisfaction if her partner began his lovemaking by reading a story to her which became gradually more pornographic in its content. One might be tempted to explain this as an Oedipal phenomenon: just as the parent read to the child in infancy, now the scenario is repeated once again. But this would not explain why it would not be equally important for the boy. Both boys and girls, after all, are read to. It shows, on the contrary, the special value of words for a woman. It is as if the relation to the man's body needs to be mediated by something, by words, just as in the deflowering ceremonies we discussed earlier, the bride's first night with her husband needs to be mediated by the symbolic reference represented by the deflowering.

What is important here is *saying*. In *All's Well that Ends Well*, Helena is looked after by the Countess of Rossillion and is secretly in love with the latter's son Bertram. The

Countess learns of this and insists that Helena tell her. She knows perfectly well who the object of her love is, so why does she insist that Helena *say* it? Once Helena has confessed, she says nothing more about it, as if the key were simply the fact that she say the words 'I love your son.' The same structure is apparent in the later scene where Helena has to name Bertram once again. She succeeds in curing the king of an affection and is thus allowed to name the man she wishes to wed. The whole scene is organized around her failing to name other men and then eventually designating Bertram: 'This is the man.' This certainly contrasts with Bertram's own position in the play: for him, it is not a question of declaring 'This is the woman,' but its contrary. He only succeeds in loving Helena once he has slept with her assuming that she was *another* woman. She only becomes desirable, then, once he has affirmed 'This is not the woman.' Leopold Stern reports on an analagous case, a man who arranged to cuckold himself with his own wife, arranging illicit meetings in a bachelor's *pied-à-terre* where he served her with port and *petits-fours*. This implies that the best way to save a marriage is to lose one's wife: if you want a marriage to last and you accept the Freudian idea that second marriages are best, there is no choice but to follow Bertram, to make the woman who was your wife not your wife in order to find her again as your wife. In terms of speech, it is of interest here to recall Reik's observation that a man frequently finds a kind of satisfaction in informing his family of the failure of his marriage, whereas a woman may be most anxious at this prospect. A female patient rationalized her failure to leave her ill-chosen husband with exactly this motive: she just could not face the moment of having to inform her father of the collapse of the marriage, even though it was clear to her and to everyone else that the father would not have been displeased to hear this.

Helena's lesson about saying also serves to dispel a popular misconception about femininity. The latter is so often equated with the desire to have children, and the fantasy image of the woman with her children around her is certainly ubiquitous. But what is even more powerful than this image of the mother with her children? Isn't it the image of the girl *telling* her partner that she is pregnant and watching his face change into the picture of happiness? The relation of maternity is thus predicated here less on the image of children than on that of speech and the transformation of the partner's facial expression. The image of the mother surrounded by her children is really more of a male fantasy anyway. Goethe's Werther falls for Lotte at the moment when he sees her dishing out slices of bread and butter to the circle of youngsters around her: this particular version of maternity is what captures his fantasy instantly. It is interesting to note here that the images of the mother recalled by men so often focus on moments of *giving*, and so rarely, outside analysis, on those of allure or concealment; the sort of accent which one woman's early memories of the visible outline of her mother's bra beneath her black sweater illustrates with precision.

Let's return to the question of the role of speech and the relation it has to the man. Certainly this is linked to love.

If a woman asks her partner where he'd like to go on holiday in the summer and he replies with a concrete destination, it would be unusual if she were to ask the same question repeatedly over the remaining months. But when she asks 'Do you love me?', it is sure that this question will be repeated. Why should the man's response, if he says 'Yes', have to be reiterated endlessly?

No doubt because what is at stake is a proof of love, the fact that love cannot be spoken once and for all. Love aims at something unconditional, absolute, which is why one response, one gesture is not enough. When a child asks its mother for various products at the supermarket, the mother might indulge the youngster. But, as all mothers know, what she gives will not be enough. The child will ask for still something else. This is no doubt the reason why there is always a little display of sweets just at the checkout and one sees so often the child's last demand at this moment. Supermarkets are alert to the unconditional nature of demand. They know that all the objects from the shelves which weigh down the mother's trolley are ultimately inadequate. The key is that in asking for something, the child's request becomes something more: as Lacan pointed out, in asking, the child puts the mother in the position of the one who can respond or not respond to the demand. This will be indicative of her love. Thus, in making the request, the specificity of the original object – the sweets – is lost: what was a demand for a particular product is transformed, via the act of speaking, into a demand for love. Which of course cannot be satisfied by sweets.

We can also observe this in the common replies to the demand for love. If a woman says to a man 'I love you', he might well reply 'Me too'. But if a man says to a woman 'I love you', she is perhaps more likely to ask for the details of *why*. 'Because of your smile.' 'And what else?' 'Because of your wit.' 'And what else?' The first thing Cleopatra says in *Antony and Cleopatra* is 'If it be love indeed, tell me how much,' and Antony wisely declines to make a comparison. Many men would fall into the trap here – 'I love you as much as . . .' – assuming that language is built to reply to the question. Since it is not, the only possible linguistic reply would involve a mistake, using language and words but indicating, via the error, the mistake in language, that something beyond words is being touched on. So, for example, to the impossible question 'How much do you love me?', the best reply might be: 'Big'.

One might conclude here with the idea that the woman continues to question because the object of love cannot be fully articulated in language: the man has to continue speaking because his words can never fully circumscribe her being. 'Tell me what it is that you love in me, but if you can do this, is that really all? Is that all I am for you?' Yet this would be to ignore the fact that, for a man, the love may be dependent on the speech itself. The love would not simply be expressed by the speech, it may *be* the speech, constructed out of the speech to the extent that all speech is a demand for love. In the frenzied epistolary activity of *Love's Labour's Lost* the men spend all their time sending messages to the women, but when it comes to actually encountering them, things are uneasy. This is a play which sets itself the task of dealing with the relation of men and women, yet it consists simply of an extended chain of wordplays, as if to indicate that this is what love relations are really all about. Letters are written in this play because that is what love is all about, producing 'a lover's discourse'. To be in love just means to go through certain literary motions. The reality of the love, in this case, is just the process itself of declaring one's love. It is as if the 'emotion', if there is one, is produced by the speech, which is logically prior. A more modern version of this wisdom is contained in the James-Lange theory that mimicry of an affective expression may secondarily produce the affect itself. The more you feign affection, the more affectionate you will become. But perhaps things are not the same for the sexes here: a woman's love might begin not when she *says* 'I love you', like the man in our example, but when she *thinks* 'I could love him.'

And how can a reply satisfy the demand for love if what a woman aims at is to be loved *for her difference*? At the end of *Pride and Prejudice* it is not Darcy who replies to Elizabeth's question, Why do you love me? She supplies the answer herself: you love me because I was different from everyone else at the ball. Or in *Love in the Afternoon*, Audrey Hepburn tries to distinguish herself from the other women in the series by her enigmatic disappearances and by refusing to disclose her name to Flanagan. She makes herself 'different' by situating herself in a series and at the same time dropping out of a series through her lack of a name. If this difference is linked to a lack of a name, how can it be named in itself? This is the reason why damaging gossip about the sexual reputation of a man often has the effect of arousing a woman's interest in him. Rather than thinking that she will be just one of a series of women seduced and then abandoned, she may think that she will be able to be different: she will enter the series in order to make the man love her for her difference. If speech itself cannot name this difference for a woman, a man's relation to the language of love has a rather particular goal: what counts for a man is to make the woman speak *to him*. Let's see what this means via another detour through the field of jealousy.

Three

The classical psychoanalytic explanation of male jealousy is that it involves an unconscious homosexual attraction to the male rival, as if the subject were saying 'It's not me that loves you, it's my wife.' Now, this sort of explanation is a bit misleading. It misinterprets the positioning of the phallus on the side of the other man as homosexuality. Rather, just as we saw in the dream of Lacan's patient, what is at stake here is the man's attempt to avoid his own deflation, the fact that his real sexual action can never match the phallic omnipotence of his fantasy. In order to understand a man's jealousy, I think, we need to focus less on the male rival than on the woman, since what a man is really jealous of is not another man but the sexuality itself of the opposite sex. A woman's sexuality, after all, is never fully directed towards a man: there is an apparent self-sufficiency which is lacking in men, despite the popular image of the 'loner', the man who does not need women. But a loner is in fact simply someone who does not need women because his link to his mother is so strong: to be everything for one's mother entails being nothing for another woman. The real loner, however, is not the man but the woman's own sexuality, the fact that her sexuality does not require a real man to articulate itself. Here again we could refer to the role of masturbation in sexual life. To illustrate this idea of jealousy, we can evoke a clinical vignette taken from the psychoanalytic literature.

A man suspects his wife of infidelity. He starts to examine her underwear microscopically, counting the number of pubic hairs deposited and trying to establish statistical correlations between an increase in the number of hairs and his wife's time spent outside the house. In other words, he does not want to know whether she is being unfaithful or not: he does not go to hire a private detective to find out. What he aims at is less a proof of his wife's fidelity than a proof of her jouissance. He wants to turn her bodily deposits, the pubic hairs, into a sign. By establishing the statistical correlations, he is trying to make her sexuality say something. When, of course, a woman's sexuality can never be translated completely into this register of language. Pubic hairs, like the planets, do not speak.

We could say that the jealousy here consists in trying to make the woman's jouissance confess, to become a sign. When the one thing that men have never been able to accept, and that they never will accept, is that womens' bodies do not speak to them. That is why men really do appreciate hysterics, even if they are always complaining about them, since hysterics are in general women whose bodies do in fact speak. Freud saw this at the start of his psychoanalytic career, that the symptoms of his hysterical patients were 'joining in the conversation', sending messages linked to repressed complexes. But there is always a side to the woman's body which does not speak and this is where the jealousy of a man is ultimately directed to.

In Italo Calvino's story 'The Adventure of a Soldier', a man is travelling in a train, seated next to a veiled woman. As the train continues its trajectory, their bodies occasionally brush against each other and the soldier becomes caught up in a game of reading, interpreting what he perceives as the signs the woman is displaying. He fixes on a part of her, 'a zone of naked skin, between the ear and the curve of her full chignon. And in that dimple beneath the ear a vein throbbed: this was the answer she was giving him, clear, heart-rending, and fleeting.' In fact, there is little evidence that the woman is doing anything but trying to remain comfortable during her train ride, yet the soldier interprets every movement, every gesture, as a sign: in other words, what he wants is perhaps less to steal a kiss than to make her body speak. Were her toying with her purse-clasp and staring out of the window 'signals to him to stop? Was it a final concession she was granting him, a warning that her patience could be tried no longer? Was it this? – Tomagra asked himself – Was it this?' We can oppose the 'Was it this' of the jealous man described above with the 'It *is* this' of the man who doesn't have any doubt. This is the dividing line between neurotic jealousy and madness, the line that separates the man who tries to make a woman's body speak and the man who *knows* that he receives messages from it. Even Calvino's soldier, at the end of the story, is far from certain.

If the object of jealousy and a key factor in the problems surrounding infidelity is the jouissance of a woman, we might well ask to what is one faithful? Freud had argued that the original sexual object for both sexes is the mother. The little boy will eventually have to change his object, from his mother to another woman, while the *sex* of his object will remain the same. But a little girl will have a more difficult task. Not only will she have to change her

61

object, from the father to another man, she will also have to change the sex of the object, from her mother to her father. There are thus two separate substitutions to be made, substitutions which, Freud admitted, are never entirely carried out: there will always be a residue or remainder from each of the operations. Theorists and scholars have been commenting on this problem for many years, but what matters in this context are less the specific vicissitudes of Freud's theories than the very simple question: if the girl's first object is the mother, why does she have to have a relation with man at all? After all, her wish to receive a child from the father, one reason she turns to him, is thwarted. Freud argued that this wish to receive a child is first represented in oral form (the fantasy image of receiving the phallus through the mouth), but surely this does not square with empirical observation. Why is it that a woman may find it easier to perform fellatio on a man she does not know than to kiss him? The Freudian argument would imply precisely the contrary. Yet even if we disagree as to the form in which this desire arises, if it is a desire ultimately disappointed, we still have to pose the question: why aren't all women homosexual?

Lacan adopted a peculiar but perfectly logical thesis here. He claimed that the only true heterosexuals were female homosexuals. One way to understand this is via the theory of narcissism. Love relations, more often than not, are constructed out of images linked to the subject's view of himself. Eduard, in Goethe's novel *Elective Affinities*, is finally convinced of the reality of his love relation with Ottilie at the moment he sees that her handwriting is exactly the same as his. Or, as Hilda wrote to her husband Stanley Spencer, 'You want me to be the most faithful copy of you that anyone could be.' Freud called this 'narcissistic object choice': one loves someone who is like oneself or who incarnates what one would want to be. In a general sense, the aim of love here is to be loved back. It's the difference between the man who feigns love in order to enter into a sexual relation and the man who enters into a sexual relation in order to procure the other's love. Despite the male stereotype, this latter stategy is hardly uncommon. The subject does his best to drag his partner into the cage of his own narcissism.

Now, Lacan's idea here is that this is not exactly the case with female homosexuals. There is the possibility of a love which is not situated only in the field of reciprocity. In other words, someone may love here without the exigency to be loved back in return. Thus a criterion for determining female homosexuality would involve reference to this idea of the service rendered to the partner, the care taken in procuring the other's jouissance. Many men, after all, take no care at all here. After obtaining some satisfaction of their own, they feel freed rather than commited. To entertain a relation with another woman would thus not be the criterion for this subjective position, and indeed, clinical examples frequently indicate that a woman's sexual relation with another woman is by no means an indication of real homosexuality. The same goes for the man here. Freud had pointed out in his discussion of the case of the female homosexual, that the sex of one's partner is not an adequate determinant of one's real sexual choice. It is not the sex of the person you sleep with which will make you a homosexual or not, despite the fact that some people who want to be homosexual think that this is the solution. To claim to be homosexual is a common alibi for not confronting certain fundamentally distinct questions. A man who experiences difficulties in being a man may claim that in fact he is a woman, erroneously equating the idea of being a woman with being homosexual. If there are supposedly only men and women, and there is a problem in being a man, the solution is to claim to be a woman. This is a big mistake. The man who experiences difficulties in being a man is not a woman but simply a man who experiences difficulties in being a man. Male homosexuals are well aware of this and do not make the confusion.

A gay man is dining with a promiscuous friend, and tells him that he is flattered that his friend can take time off from his amatory schedule which is occupied exclusively with women. The friend replies that he is in fact still occupied with a woman, at which point his dining companion storms out of the restaurant, putting an end to the friendship there and then. The reply was disastrous as it made exactly the mistake that we have been discussing, to identify 'to be a woman' and 'to be homosexual'.

If Freud's arguments about the Oedipal development of the girl pose the question we evoked above – why is the relation with the man necessary – the field of female homosexuality complicates matters even further. Presumably we are dealing here with the relation of a woman to a woman. But things are not so simple. Freud's patient (known as the 'female homosexual') gives us an example. She displays a motherly attitude in relation to the children around her and then, at a particular moment, starts to act the courtly lover with an older woman, a *demi-mondaine*, sending her flowers, following her around and so forth. What is it that precipitates this dramatic change in her behaviour? Lacan singles out as a key factor the pregnancy of the young lady's mother. She had situated her existence up till this point in a love relation with her father which took the form of waiting for an imaginary child from him. Hence her motherly behaviour. But now, she confronts the reality of a child which is given not to her but to her mother. And what does the young lady do? She starts to court the older woman in a conspicuous fashion, knowing full well that her father is incensed by this behaviour. In other words, when she faces a disappointment in the register of love from the father, she becomes the lover herself. Sending flowers, waiting on the older woman's beck and call and all the other activities which put her in the position not of the object of love but in that of the lover. She is trying to show her father, Lacan argued, what a true love is, a love which is directed to a woman, someone who, in a sense, doesn't have anything (for example, a child). She is loving the Lady for what she hasn't got, just as her father ought to have loved her. The clue to this interpretation lies in the details of the episode which precipitates her in an attempt at suicide.

She is with her Lady in the street when she encounters her father. He gives her a furious glare, but this is not the real trigger to the episode. She expected, in a sense, that she would meet her father since it was a neighbourhood he frequented. The key is in the fact that the Lady then asked her who that man was and when she informs her that it was her father, the Lady became angry with her as well. In other words, it was no longer possible to sustain the relation with the Lady as a performance directed to her father as the spectator, since now the Lady was *herself* occupying the father's place. This shows us how a relation between two women is not limited to the actors materially present: as a demonstration addressed to the father, there is a third party, and we see this also in the fact that sometimes a woman engaged in a sexual relation with another woman will feel the presence of an invisible witness. This witness, if we accept Freud's case as a paradigm, will be linked to the father.

Ernest Jones was alert to this dimension. He discussed those female homosexuals who seem to aim at enjoying their own femininity in another woman 'at the hand of an unseen man', the paternal figure he assumed was 'incorporated' within them. Whilst we may disagree with the idea of an 'incorporation', the presence of the third party is indeed frequently discernable, materialized in the form of a man who is actually present or even in the form of a photograph or an item of furniture associated with the paternal register. It does not have to be a real man and certainly not the real father.

Vita Sackville-West offers another illustration here of the relation of female lovers to their witness. She gallivants around with Violet Trefusis dressed as a man – Julian – and yet rather than changing back into more feminine clothes well before her arrival back at the family home, she waits till literally the last minute, thus introducing the possibility that she might be caught by her father. The activity with Violet thus shares this dimension of a demonstration directed to an addressee who is not physically present. Virginia Woolf's letter to Vita, *Orlando*, was indeed originally conceived as a story of 'two women, poor, solitary, at the top of a house . . . Also old men listening in the room over the way. Sapphism is to be suggested.' The presence of the male spectator is thus a part of the scenario of the two women. We could read Virginia's last sentence here as an imperative rather than as an evocation: the Sapphism suggests itself due to the presence of the 'old men'. We see here also the reason why Virginia Woolf could never have a Room of her Own: her father was always in there with her. The solitary woman's attic is also the space where the father listens and watches till eternity.

Whatever critical approaches one adopts to *Orlando*, there's no denying that it contains the most dazzling first word of any work of literature in English: 'He'. The reading public knew perfectly well that the book would be a sort of biography of Vita Sackville-West and awaited its publication with baited breath, expecting to find details of the subject's convoluted and scandalous love life, particularly her relations with other women. And yet what a surprise greeted them on the printed page: the masculine pronoun in all its simplicity, separated from the rest of the sentence by a carefully chosen dash. In a sense, the arrow that the book fired was contained within that one word.

To continue the parallel with Freud's case history, we find a similar disappointment from the father just before the invention of Vita's 'Julian' persona. He had just made formal the establishment of an affair with another woman, Olive Rubens. Thus her flaunting of Julian may be seen as a defiance of the father, and it is surely no accident that she chooses as the title of her first novel born out of her relation with a woman the word *Challenge*. Commentators tend to be overwhelmed by the impressive figure of Vita's mother and to explain the homosexual dynamic in those terms, neglecting this critical importance of the father. Yet when Violet, someone who knew a thing or two about Vita, was moved to compile a list of what England meant for her beloved, she summed up:

Long Barn
your books
your garden
Knole
your father
people you like

It is the father rather than the mother who features in this list of things indispensible to Vita.

Another factor is important here: Harold, Vita's husband-to-be, informs her just before the start of her affair with Violet that he has a venereal disease. In other words, the relation with the woman takes place in the shadow of the man's being robbed of his manliness. This is in no way opposed to his attraction for her. It is clear that Harold was maintained as a straw man throughout their long and rather successful marriage, something which Violet was never to understand. Her reproaches to Vita for her love for the 'H.N. fiction' failed to register the fact that Harold was loved precisely for this fictive quality, the fact of not being a 'real man'.

If one has the opportunity to eavesdrop on the conversation of elderly ladies after church on the nature of Christ, one is struck by the way in which he is described with all the features of the ideal lover. Indeed, in medieval preaching books and manuals of instruction, he is frequently depicted as a lover knight, one who dies for the sake of his Lady in order to win her love. He endured, we learn, the torments of the Passion to win man's love, and one eccentric fourteenth-century sermon even compares Christ to a cuckold, in the sense that he endeavours to win back his Lady due to her unfaithfulness. Christ may thus be an ideal man, but at the same time he is not a 'real man'. A recent compilation of interviews with nuns makes this clear: however much he is adored, he is consistently depicted as a failure. 'In the world's terms', one nun tells us, 'Jesus was a pretty dismal failure.' But it is exactly this failure which makes of him the focus of a woman's love: he is loved, we could say, not for his Resurrection, but for his Passion. And this is what Violet could not understand, even though she would subsequently bind herself, in a tempestuous way, to a man very much like Harold, Denys Trefusis.

As for the relation of Vita to her husband Harold, it would be difficult, as we have said, not to see their marriage as largely successful. It is curious to note that if we take this union of Vita and Harold as a paradigm, it consists precisely in the marriage of two homosexuals. Psychoanalytic literature is filled with explanations of why marriages dissolve, but there are hardly any discussions of why some marriages actually work. In a sense, this is a much more difficult question. Milton claimed that divorce, not marriage, was what comes closest to the spirit of 'peace and love': it is divorce, he argues, not sex, which is the fundamental human act of release, and not to dare divorce is man's real infirmity. Indeed, in his commonplace book, under 'Marriage', it says 'see Divorce'. Swift, a little irked by this conception, commented that Milton had only said this because, as everybody knew, when he wrote it, 'he had a Shrew for his wife'. In the analytic camp, Edmund Bergler once wrote a book called *Divorce Won't Help*, a title which sets out in itself an intriguing agenda and invites us to meditate upon the unchronicled history of one of civilization's best-kept secrets: the happy marriage. The verses have yet to be written which set out the stakes for this perpetual conflict over Eden: Milton vs. Bergler.

Elizabeth Taylor no doubt uses the same commonplace book as Milton, but her relation to marriage and divorce is quite singular. If she made her name in the cinema, she is now famous less for her movies than for her systematic divorces. In a sense, she made a career out of ending her marriages. The key, however, is that she doesn't complain about all this: she complains about other things instead (weight, narcotics . . .). If one is doomed to repeat one's destiny, the mistakes, for example, of one's parents and grandparents, Elizabeth Taylor offers a truly psychoanalytic resolution to one's fate. If she repeats the same thing over and over again in her marriages and divorces, she is following her destiny, but without complaining, without turning it into a tragedy. Seneca said that one has two choices in life: to be led by fate or to be dragged by fate. That is, to repeat the same things and complain of them, to live them as tragedy, or, to repeat the same things but with some enthusiasm, to make one's career and one's life out of them, something that has more of a comic than a tragic accent. Seneca would have been impressed with

Elizabeth Taylor's assumption of her destiny, even if the luxuriant tastes of the star and her fine collection of gems might not have appealed to his Stoic vision. The question may now be asked: were her husbands led, like Elizabeth, or dragged by fate? There are books called *The Wives of Henry VIII* but none called *The Husbands of Elizabeth Taylor*. Given the prospects of the Taylor husbands on the eve of their weddings, Hobhouse's description of Lord Byron at a similar moment might supply the title of the projected volume: 'The Bridegroom More and More Less Impatient'. To find a real psychoanalytic explanation for this lack of symmetry would genuinely contribute to knowledge about the sexes. Why are series of men always so much less exciting? And who can name the husbands of Zsa Zsa Gabor?

Four

The relationship of two women does not necessarily exclude the reference, however hidden, to a man and it is probable that this man is to be identified with the father. Thus the giving up of men may well take place in the shadow of a relation to one man who is not given up. This shows us how the Freudian argument which we took as our point of departure in the last section, the suggestion that a woman's sexuality involves the subtraction of the man, needs to be complicated. The absence of the man is still linked to the motif of the father. It means that the notions of presence and absence need to be explored in greater detail, if the physical absence of one man may be predicated on the unreal presence of another. This is perhaps one of the key problems of feminine sexuality, the effort to give a sense to an absence. It indicates the importance of questions of *meaning* and *explanation* to any discussion of female sexuality. This theme is elaborated with an unusual clarity in the work of Mary Shelley. We can take as our example not the well-known *Frankenstein* but rather the short novel *Mathilda*, only published in 1959 and somewhat neglected in the Shelley literature.

The book concerns a young woman who lives in the expectation of the return of her father, departed to the Continent after the tragic death of his wife. When he finally returns the father and daughter enjoy a short period of bliss, Mathilda at last receiving all the love from him that she had dreamt of for so long. But this love becomes concrete and the father indicates that it is somewhat more than platonic. Unable to face the reality of this desire, he departs once again, committing suicide before his daughter can catch up with him to prevent this. Readers of *Frankenstein* may note the structural similarity of the chase motif here with the hare and tortoise race of Frankenstein and the monster. It indicates that the two players are situated in incommensurable spaces: it is not possible for them both to come into the same place even if they may have contingent encounters at various points along the way. I will return to this theme later on, but let's first examine the development in *Mathilda*.

Leaving her estate, the young woman travels north and secludes herself in a small house far from civilization. Her life there is interrupted by the attentions of a young poet, Woodville, whom she separates from rather swiftly. Commentators on the text usually focus on his resemblance to the poet Shelley, yet it seems that the key to Woodville's appearance in the story is precisely the fact that he is given up. He is introduced only to be made to disappear. And now Mathilda, resigned to death, can tell us that her true partner is solitude, but a solitude with a very precise meaning. It means 'not being with the father', as if this 'not being with' is *itself* a partner of the subject. 'In solitude', she says, 'I shall be thine.' The state of *not being with the father* is given an erotic value in itself, and privileged over *'being with a man'*. This is by no means always the case with a woman: many women choose 'to be with a man' but at the same time as 'to be with the father'.

This latter situation is a recipe for trouble as the two propositions are clearly contradictory.

Mathilda, in contrast to such women, chose the other alternative: she accepted as her partner not a man but the absence of a man. Rather than protesting the space left by his absence, she sexualizes it. This brings us to a crucial choice for a woman, the choice of how she is going to value the space in question. Let's say that there are at least two alternatives. If one lacks something, one can endeavour to obtain it and one might suppose that someone else has got it, the man for example. Result: the warfare that often characterizes the life of a couple. The precious object is on the side of the man, and, if this is accepted by a woman, she may well bind herself to him and adore him for this. And battle with him at the same time.

But another path is open here, a very different one. A woman makes the decision to renounce men and to seclude herself in a religious order with the motto '*Thou shalt not have*'. Rather than attempting to have, she chooses to situate her existence beneath this banner of not having. But this giving up, she says, is itself a 'precious jewel'. As another nun tells us, 'Sometimes I've scurried around looking for the treasure in the religious life, whereas the treasure was the transaction. I sold everything. I gave away everything. And now everything belongs to me.' The jewel is not situated in another space but *is constructed from the space of not having itself*, in the same way that a crystal will emerge from a saturated solution. Saturation here means sexualization. The crystal, the jewel, will thus not emerge if the space is not sexualized in the right way.

74

The first speaker continues: 'The end in itself is not destitution. It's a having – I was going to say 'without possessing' – but it's a having without being possessed.' If we take the slip of the tongue seriously, we have a beautiful formulation of a current of feminine sexuality. To give up everything, to give up having, is not to make oneself destitute because the giving up itself is a form of having something. The woman might not possess something, what some psychoanalysts might interpret rudely as 'lack of the penis', but she certainly has something. The difference in the two feminine positions here would be between the woman who situates the jewel on the side of the man – which means that she is not going to give up men – and the woman who gives the empty space of not possessing a sexual value, a value which will itself materialize the jewel. Men, in the everyday sense of the word, are no longer necessary.

This problem of having and not having is somewhat different for men. We could say that having for a man is always based on the possibility of not having: having means owning with all the risks that this involves. In contemporary culture, the car alarm illustrates this structure very neatly. When your sleep is interrupted by a car alarm, the last thing you think of is that a car is really being stolen. Car thieves, after all, are Darwinian: they have adapted to the existence in their habitat of alarm systems. They know how to steal a car quietly. The alarm itself rings out solely in order to remind us that what we have is always situated in the shadow of not having, that what we own is always based on the fragile foundation of not owning. As St Paul insisted, man must have as though he had not, possess as though he did not possess. The contemporary icons of masculinity show us this clearly. Rap stars sing of their exploits and of how many policemen they have eliminated, but when the suspicion arises that one such star may actually have perpetrated the deed in question, a whole battery of lawyers make their appearance to prove that it was in fact someone else who pulled the trigger, a bystander or the bodyguard. Everyone is supposed to know that what the man claims to have done, he has not in fact done. His maleness is theatre.

For a woman, as we have seen, having is a different story. It may also take the form of a 'being to', which is the simple sense of the verb 'to have'. Having something means that it is to you. Thus a female version of 'having' would be 'belonging to', which entails, of course, a giving up. As Reik pointed out, in love it is not possible to really possess someone: the most one can do is to belong to them. To belong to someone means giving up something. But what the nuns showed us was the way in which the giving up itself constituted a new form of having, one which goes beyond the idea of belonging to a real man.

Another version would revolve around the importance of a brother. A male sibling may be the object of identification or set the pattern for a girl's choice of partner due to the place he occupies for the mother. If the mother gives a key place to the male child, he is bound to exert an unconscious attraction for the sister due to the dependence of her desire on the desire of the mother. But what is interesting here is the way in which a girl will often want her brother to *do something*, even to the extent of renouncing a career for herself once he is successful. What distinguishes this sort of structure from the simple and all too common repression by a family of a girl's potential is the satisfaction she may feel at the sacrifice. It is the brother who *has* in her place. Any tainting of the image of the brother can then have devastating consequences, as it will concern the sister quite directly. It is received wisdom that a sister may search for a new lover the moment she hears of her brother's relation with a woman. This observation, grounded on the supposition of jealousy, is not, however, strictly true: it is just as likely that the sister will search for a lover once the brother's relation with a woman has just *ended*. The collapse of the brother's romance may evoke his not-having, and so the sister turns to another man to reformulate the whole problematic: for example, as we just noted, by interpreting 'to have' as 'to be to', to belong to another man.

A young girl moves with her family to a new apartment. In her brother's room there is a hook in the middle of the ceiling. She knows immediately that the hook is destined for her and becomes haunted with the image of her lifeless body hanging from it. In her dreams and associations, it appears as if the hook is the way, for her, of formulating that her brother had something which she didn't have. It was the only explicit difference between the two empty rooms. The problem is that to have this herself meant her own sacrifice, her own disappearance, a subjective position echoed systematically in her adult life where she would continuously stage her own vanishing, failing to turn up for rendezvous, work and so on. The powerful image of the hanging girl thus gave the matrix of her relations, always revolving around the idea of being missed, of making herself absent, in all senses of the word. In her love relations, she would become lifeless and her body felt to her like a corpse. Thus, confronted with the emergence of love, she could only operate with the position she gave herself in childhood, in relation to the family's giving the room with the hook to her brother and the logic which she constructed around this image. It was her way of making sense of the brother's having something in relation to the desires of the parents. Of course, the story is more complex here, but it illustrates the particular sensitivity to having and not having in its relations to the sibling.

The question of having may indeed take on an infinite number of forms. Someone may spend their life going from one doctor to another convinced that they 'have' something, resolute in their obliviousness to the negative opinions of medicine. The question may persist even if a medical problem is indeed found: a woman systematically refers to the removal of her four cysts when in fact only three had been operated on. A man claims that he always chooses a woman as his partner when she has four attributes: a certain figure, a certain colour hair, a certain tone of voice ... but he can never 'remember' the fourth attribute. The woman, for him, has something which he cannot name. For a man, this having often takes the form of some unnameable physical feature, whereas, as we have seen, for a woman it may appear in the guise of a 'doing', a purposefulness. A daughter may always remain true to the conviction that her father is a great man who deserves a better fate. Charlotte Brontë could never accept the fact, it seems, that the writer Thackeray was not a 'man with a mission'. However much he denied this calling, she persisted in maintaining him in the place of a man who was going to 'do' something.

We see a contrasting illustration of the man's relation to having in *The Merchant of Venice*. Bassanio must choose between the three caskets to win the fair Portia. The choice is simple: gold, silver or lead. And each casket carries a different legend. For gold: 'Who chooseth me, shall gain what many men desire.' For silver: 'Who chooseth me, shall get as much as he deserves.' For lead: 'Who chooseth me, must give and hazard all he hath.' Bassanio, of course, chooses the lead casket but what, after all, does he have to give? Nothing, since his riches are simply the result of a loan from his friend Antonio. He gives literally what he does not have, he hazards what he hasn't got. In fact, we could say that Bassanio makes the wrong choice. In the gold casket is a skull, in the silver casket a note indicating the foolishness of the one who has chosen silver, and in the lead casket a portrait of the beautiful Portia. In one sense, the man who chooses gold has made the right choice: he has understood that beyond the beautiful image of Portia there is simply the brute object of a death's head, what ultimately lies beyond the register of the vanities. To choose lead and find the beautiful image implies only that one is duped by love, believing that at the core of the partner's being there is a beautiful object and not a death's head. His prize is no more and no less than an image. Bassanio, then, is the real lover if, as the poet had reminded us earlier in the play, love is what makes you blind.

Whether this blindness afflicts Portia is another question, but, as Reik pointed out many years ago, the riddle of the caskets forms part of a chain implicit in the drama. Portia is the character who puts men to the test throughout the play, from the challenge of the caskets to the courtroom scene where she impersonates a lawyer and the episode of the rings which closes the play. She has given a ring to Bassanio earlier on, and he has pledged not to part with it. Portia disguises herself as a lawyer in order to save Antonio, the man who had supplied the money to Bassanio to finance his courting activities. And now, still disguised, she demands the ring as token of his gratitude. He gives it to her and then, later on, undisguised, Portia takes up the issue of the missing ring with him. So fond is she of putting men through ordeals that, as Reik noted, it is as if Portia herself becomes the puzzle, the enigma which has to be resolved. This point may help to shed some light on the old problem: why do princesses in fairy tales spend so much time setting riddles to young men? The answer may be Reikian: the princess sets so many riddles because, ultimately, she aims to be the riddle herself. The facility with which Portia engages in this task is in marked contrast with that of the man. It is amazing how untalented men are at being enigmatic, at becoming riddles: if a man wears sunglasses at a dinner is it worth giving him the time of day? Or if he dissimulates, how long does it really take before one is aware of the truth? To maintain the dimension of the riddle, for a woman, is to sustain desire, to keep the man from knowing too much and so guarantee that desire continues. The problem is that the choice between two options for a woman here is not always easy: finding the right person not to understand one, to respect the riddle, or the wrong person to understand. Perhaps the person who understands is *always* the wrong person, and the problem with the right person is that, very simply, he doesn't understand.

If not having for a woman can create a space where the presence of men is no longer required, her solitude may be something very specific and fundamentally different from that of a man. Being alone for a man is perhaps linked to another problematic. When Byron refers to the 'solitude of kings', the key to understanding the solitude may be in the reference to kings. After all, most countries can only have one of them at a time. Does this indicate that male solitude is more linked to hatred than to love? Let's take an example from the case of a male neurotic discussed by Leclaire. This man's memories seem to focus on the single image of a battlefield just after the war has ended. He is walking across the desolate space trying to reach his regiment and he sees in the distance another solitary figure walking in his direction. The war is over and so there is no danger. But all the same, if the other soldier is a German, what will he do? As they pass each other, might the other man turn and shoot him out of fear? Even if he has no hostile wishes against this other man, the latter might assume that he, on the contrary, does. It is not possible to calculate what is going on in the mind of the other figure. And so, with this unbearable anxiety, they cross paths, in silence. Now, this vignette is exemplary. It shows the way in which man is overpowered by his hostility for his fellow man and how, in the vast empty space of the battlefield, the lonely encounter of two men introduces, unavoidably, the signification of mortality. They pass each other in silence and we might conjecture that in a similar situation, if the soldiers had been female, they would have struck up a conversation. But men are rendered mute by this fundamental hostile relation to their counterpart. A woman, on the contrary, when harbouring enormous hostility to another woman, may sometimes resort to an elegant tactic: she will turn her into her best friend. Men's problems here are handled with more clumsiness and negative sentiments are manifest. Everyone who lives in the big city knows this: the only time you ever get to talk to your neighbour is when you are siding with him against the neighbour next but one. In the court of Queen Elizabeth, the only thing that kept Raleigh and Cecil from each other's throats was their temporary alliance against Essex: once he was out of the way, there wasn't a courtier next but one and there was no choice but to destroy each other.

We could also cite, in this context, two famous encounters between men which were characterized by the same sort of paralysis. When the mathematician Sylvester visited Poincaré at his apartment near the Luxembourg Gardens in Paris, he was completely mute as he stared at the famous French thinker who had just opened the door. And Bergson, when he finally had the opportunity to meet William James, simply stood there in silence like his American counterpart. When he at last managed a 'Bonjour', James could do nothing but reply immediately with the request to hear Bergson's views on the problem of religion!

It is not simple admiration but the necessity of the destruction of the other which causes the muteness in these examples. We see this elaborated in the life of a man famous for his seclusion and his apparent ability to live without women: Schopenhauer, the philosopher who cited Malebranche, Descartes, Leibniz, Spinoza and Kant as kindred spirits in their resolute celibacy. One has the impression that closeness for this man was ruled out by the exigency to obliterate anyone else who might be king. When he was given a lecturing post at Berlin in 1820, the philosopher Hegel was at the height of his fame. Yet Schopenhauer nonetheless insisted on holding his course at exactly the same time as his rival's most popular seminar. When it was suggested to him that he change his timetable, he chose rather to resign from the university altogether. This sort of reaction is indicative of the problem of situating oneself in the Oedipal structure, and it is no accident that the philosopher was constantly to change and rewrite the dedication to his father of the second edition of his central work, although the latter had already been dead for many years. This inability to formulate a satisfactory dedication shows the impossibility for Schopenhauer of giving a proper symbolic form to his relation with the father: he is thus left in the field of imaginary battles. In the margins of his lecture notebooks, instead of finding doodles one finds derisive comments about his professors: 'idiot', 'sophist', 'drivel'. His solitude may be seen as a consequence of the aggressive nature of his relation to the register of the father: he chose the Will rather than the pacifying effect of the Idea. And in the place of the human partner, the philosopher put something else. In his study, alongside the portraits of Kant, Shakespeare, Goethe and Descartes, were pictures of dogs he had loved. 'I would not want to live', he said, 'if dogs did not exist.' This male abdication of human commerce is thus very different from the solitude of a woman: it has its roots in a failure to resolve the problematic relation with the father whereas the woman's seclusion shows, on the contrary, a form of resolution.

Psychoanalysts often claim that the boy's Oedipal structure will be nicely resolved once he has succeeded in taking the place of the father in an untroubled way. But the real question here is not simply the concern with what paternity consists of, but the inquiry into the meaning of being a son. It's true that these questions are ultimately two sides to the same coin, but there is still much interest in distinguishing them from a certain perspective. This is the dividing line between so many currents in the history of religion: of course, there is the problem of the nature of the deity, but this always involves the consideration of the question 'What is it to be a son?' The exact sense in which Christ is the 'son' of God or the question of the identity of the authentic heir to Muhammad have divided religious empires for centuries. To reduce the complexities of a religion to the motif of paternity, as many analytic writers have done, is to miss the point. After all, isn't the decisive thing about religious systems precisely the fact that they have *made a decision* about what paternity consists of: Christianity, Islam and Judaism all have answers here. What they *disagree* on, both between each other and within themselves, is the nature of sonship and inheritance. And in psychoanalysis, after all, each male subject, regardless of whether he has children, speaks not as a father but as a son. Religions, for their part, offer different formulations of this one basic question.

It is interesting that in the so-called 'golden' period in

the history of Rome from the end of the first to the end of the second century, no emperor was the son of his predecessor. The moment that a son does take this place, things get a bit out of hand. Marcus Aurelius' son Commodus behaved so badly that commentators were forced to explain the discrepancy between saintly father and corrupt son by an appeal to the infidelity of his wife Faustina. But this is not necessary. There is no need to suppose that she slept with a gladiator: on the contrary, it is precisely Marcus Aurelius' saintliness that accounts for the outrages of a Commodus. What is not symbolized for the father will emerge in all its rawness in the life of the son. The horrific images of bodily dismemberment that kept the Stoic emperor awake at night simply became realized with the son, showing that a central problem for any son is how to assume the darker elements in the life of the father. Christ's sacrifice may be interpreted in a similar way: this is an idea which runs from Gnostic thought to Hegel and Lacan, that Christ suffered not to save mankind but to save God. It is the problem of transmission which the son has to confront. He may identify with certain ideal features of the father's life but what is he supposed to do with the traces of the father's repressed enjoyment? The answer to this question will determine the way in which each male subject assumes his position as a son.

We have seen how the idea of the man being absent from the sexual life of a woman may be interpreted in many ways, none of which is reducible to the simple fact of his not being there. We might venture the hypothesis here that a part of feminine sexuality consists exactly in this effort of finding different ways of formulating the man's absence. It is a curious and striking fact that the literature of so many women writers may tell us a great deal about love relations with a man, about emotions, about passions, but *it will not tell us what the man looks like.* This is much rarer in male literature, perhaps the most famous example being Prevost's *Manon Lescaut,* where a woman who is barely described becomes the centre of so many love adventures. Men have always privileged, on the contrary, physical details of the woman who is loved: witness the one hundred sonnets written by Cornezano on the eyes of his mistress. But why is it that in the 8,000 letters of Juliette Drouet to Victor Hugo there is not one single reference to the colour of his hair?

Let us take an example from Jane Austen here, a writer who is no stranger to our theme of sexuality's divorce from the presence of a man. Her rejection of male suitors is well known, but her books show us a detail which has so far escaped the attention of critics. What happens when a man enters the parlour in a novel by Jane Austen? The answer is a very simple one: *he leaves.* He leaves and his absence is left enigmatic and unexplained until his reasons are made known. The most striking example perhaps would be the departure of Colonel Brandon in *Sense and Sensibility.* He leaves suddenly without an explanation and the characters go through a number of scenarios which might account for this strange action. We could put this into correspondence with the famous Bath episode in Austen's life where the authoress is mightily affected, almost swooning, at the news that her father has decided to relocate to the latter city. It is another example of a man deciding to go somewhere. Contrast this to the fact that Jane Austen was someone who did not go very far from home: she preferred the seclusion of her sitting room. This helps us to explain the mystery of the attraction of many women to soldiers. Why have these figures so often served as the objects of a girl's daydreams? The immediate explanation would lie in their gallantry and the romantic nature of the soldier's uniform. But doormen at hotels are also gallant and also wear a smart uniform and yet they are less frequently used as the prop of fantasy. It can't be the uniform, so perhaps it is the courage and manliness shown by these subjects in time of war? But again, women know perfectly well what war consists of: waiting in trenches, combat at a distance, an unseen enemy. The answer must lie not in the uniform or the battlefield but in the fact that, contrary to a hotel doorman, a soldier is someone who is always just about to leave. As Austen shows us, this is a sort of precondition for a man's taking on a privileged value.

We could ask at this point, What is a man for Jane Austen? The first answer would be: someone who leaves. But what we need to stress, however, is not simply the reality of the departure. What matters is that a man is someone who leaves but then whose absence is finally *explained*. We find out why Colonel Brandon left, as is the case for the other initially mysterious excursions. A man is thus someone who leaves and whose absence is explained. Let us propose another hypothesis here: that a current of feminine sexuality may consist, in part, in formulating dif-ferent responses, albeit explanations, for the departure of the man. What this means in practical terms is that a woman will have a different use for the imagination than a man. It is a cliché to say that little girls are more imaginative than little boys, but there is some truth in the remark if we interpret the 'more' in the right way. We could contrast the woman's imagination with the man's equivalent: the coarse charms of the amusement arcade. It is very rare to see women in these noisy places and in a sense the machines take the place of the imagination for the man, or more precisely, they occupy the same structural place. The man remains married to some concrete, noisy form of enjoyment (no doubt linked to his penis) whereas the woman has a rather different partner, something more silent than a pinball machine. Men's imagination is contracted to the concern of why things go up and down. Even a genius like Leonardo da Vinci had this preoccupation in mind in his attempts to design a flying machine, and his practical jokes would involve such treats as inflating an animal bladder to the size of a room. A car, of course, is a more complicated piece of machinery, but it is still the same question. Men's obsession with cars is often explained as a thirst for control over powerful machines, but if this were the case, why don't we have a TV series *Crane Driver*? What matters is understanding *how* these bits of machinery work, and the anxiety of a small boy on experiencing his first erections should leave no one in doubt as to the gravity of this question.

We have argued that for a woman, the absence of the father (or lover) may be central to her sexuality, as if a part of the sexuality is constructed out of the empty space left by his departure. Into this empty space comes the imagination and into this empty space comes the idea of a partner. This is perhaps the reason why women make such gifted mystery writers: they are sensitive to the many different ways of encoding or ciphering something that is missing.

And it also explains, perhaps, what the press have expended so much ink trying to figure out. Why is it that the most beautiful, the most photographed, the most sought-after woman in the world got herself engaged to an oddball magician? Aside from his fortune, it has proven difficult for many commentators to provide a good answer for Claudia Schiffer's choice. But the attraction of David Copperfield is a perfectly logical one. He is a magician, and perhaps not just any magician but The Magician, the most celebrated and, arguably, talented one around today. In other words, he is someone who can appear and disappear: that is literally his job. And, crucially, his absences are left enigmatic. They can provide a constant space for interpretation, and one can bet, very safely, that he hasn't told Claudia how he does it. When Reik said many years ago, and for different reasons, that what a woman wants is a magician, he was really on to something.

Lacan says at a certain point that the partner of a woman is solitude. Now, if we follow the argument sketched out above, this solitude may, in some cases, be interpreted as the libidinalization of 'not being with the father'. But what about the term *'partner'*? How might one interpret this expression? We may note first of all that it designates something more general than 'man' or 'lover'. Friend perhaps? It is clear that often women search for a friend beyond the phallic register, someone they can be with and talk to without an overt sexual relation. And of course, given the nature of men, such a desire will produce problematic relationships, to say the least. It is interesting that Mary Shelley's *Frankenstein* opens with a reference to the narrator's need for a friend. Although the narrator is, strictly speaking, 'masculine' it would be unjust to read this book as being about anything else than a woman's adventure. The creature, after all, is introduced as a partner of its creator and it strives, in its own way, to find just this, as we see in its wish to have a mate. What the book shows us is *the impossibility of the creator to assume its creature*. All the main characters who are introduced into the narrative eventually meet a grim fate, as if Shelley is systematically running through all possible partners of the subject and demonstrating their inadequateness. Like *Mathilda*, it is a narrative of the successive exhaustion of partners and it is surely no accident that later in her life Mary Shelley was to write a book entitled *The Last Man*.

Her own history mirrors this structure, notably in her tragic loss of so many children. Even with little Percy, her only child to survive beyond infancy, her letters show her inability to assume this aspect of her own creation. In a sense he became her symptom, the element that her life was reduced to and about which she would never stop wondering, Why isn't he more like his father? His mediocrity became her puzzle. It appears that she had difficulty in accepting him as the Percy that he was, just as the creator in *Frankenstein* cannot reconcile himself with his own creation. One might hypothesize that the problem for Mary was assuming the place of the mother, just as the problem for the poet Shelley was to situate himself beneath the insignia of the father. Note the way in which he falls ill after the birth of all his children. The famous controversy over the so-called 'Neapolitan charge' – an infant whose origins within the Shelley household were once much debated by scholars – is merely symptomatic of the poet's uneasy relation to paternity.

The problem of assuming one's creation illustrates the centrality of the question of who or what one's partner is. We see this in Mary's relations with the poet Shelley. She arranges their first romantic meetings in a very particular place: by the grave of her mother in St Pancras' churchyard. Her relations with the man are played out literally in the place of the mother, just as in *Mathilda* the daughter yearns to be loved by her father exactly as he had loved the mother: to take her place. This is not as obvious as it seems. One may compare it with the man's relation to 'taking the place of'. If a girl's mother is away, she may well wish to cook dinner *just like* her mother cooks dinner, but a boy may want to cook it *better*. There is a difference between 'taking the place of' in the sense of 'going further than' and 'taking the place of' in the sense of 'coming into a place'. For Mary, coming into this place is no easy task. Many women, likewise, are constantly amazed that they are married. Even years after the marriage itself, they are on a bus and the thought suddenly hits them 'I'm married'. This shows that going into the place of the mother is not, contrary to what many theorists have argued, something natural or even automatic. And likewise, that the register of the maternal must be distinguished from that of motherhood itself. These two dimensions are nearly always confused in psychological discussions: their separation is seen clearly, however, in the fact that the most maternal of women, the famous nurses and teachers of history, have most often been women without children. This would indicate, contrary to the popular identification, that perhaps motherhood and the maternal are ultimately two mutually exclusive terms.

For some women, motherhood means literally a loss of femininity. After her daughter's marriage, Madame de Sévigné devoted most of her life to repeated attempts to dissuade her from becoming pregnant. She contrasted the beautiful image of her daughter with the disfigurement she associated with childbirth. We could say that the question 'What is it to be a woman?' became focused, after her marriage, on the daughter: she became the site of the mother's terrible inquiry into femininity, a weight which any daughter will find difficult to bear. It is surely no accident that the daughter's side of the correspondence was destroyed and that she chose to absent herself from the funeral of her mother. If the daughter becomes the 'Other Woman', the place of the question, for her mother, the effects are not less than tempestuous, returning to her in the form, for example, of a complete paralysis in relations with men or the nightmares which disturb her sleep.

The psychoanalyst Karen Horney had a peculiar idea about the passage from daughter to mother. She thought that since marriage involves 'taking the place of' the parents, there must be a price to be paid. If so many neurotic symptoms are based on the feelings of guilt linked to usurping a parent, how on earth can one get away with such an astonishing trespass as a marriage? Horney's answer is simple: the price you pay for the marriage is its unhappiness. A marriage must be an unhappy one, since suffering is the condition under which one can continue to flout the prohibition against incest, of going into the place of the mother or the father.

For Mary Shelley the question is slightly different, although it is exactly this passage into the place of the mother which poses a problem. Her father had taught her to read and spell her name by having her trace her mother's inscription on the latter's tombstone at St Pancras, but she would never assume this place: instead, *writing itself* became a way for her to articulate the impossibility of this passage. Her true partner, perhaps, like Mathilda's, was solitude, which implies an absence of children. We recall the vision she has after the death of her daughter Clara: 'I saw myself desolate and alone – my William . . . gone . . . beloved Shelley vanished'. Her son William is to die soon after and in her ensuing depression she writes *Mathilda*, a book about being alone, but in the specific sense we have discussed of not being with the father.

It is interesting to note that Mary intended the profits from the sale of this book to go to her father, William Godwin, who had just lost a lawsuit over a rent. The day she finds out about this she takes up the writing of the book again. It is a labour of love, but one addressed to a father who has nothing. What kind of a man is this who, furious at the elopement of his daughter and the poet Shelley, refuses all intercourse with them except for his requests for money from the poet? The father is not one who gives here, although this may be what is expected of him. A little girl may refuse the gift of a toy from her mother and only accept it when it comes from the right place: the father as the one who gives. This is perhaps the reason why Thomas More's first wife was happy to receive a set of false jewels from him: she was just as happy as if they had been genuine because they took on their real value as something that is given by the man. It is thus the envelope rather than the letter which counts, the jewel box rather than the jewels. We see this also in the way in which a man might fetishize a piece of a woman's clothing or a lock of her hair, whereas a woman may give a special value to gifts. In contrast with women, when men receive presents, it is rarely the thought that counts.

With Mary, the attempt to direct the projected profits of the book to Godwin represents an attempt to give something back to the father, loving him for what he hasn't got. Godwin is not a father who says 'I love thee', but rather one who says 'Give me cash', just as in *Mathilda* the father's actual statement of love means much more than the daughter bargained for. The problem is in assuming what a father's love might consist of: perhaps it is not altogether surprising that later in her life Mary was to turn to another woman for a different form of love. At the horizon of the father's affection, there is always something else, perhaps the love directed not to her but to her mother. This means that the most passionate demand for the fidelity of a man will always have the infidelity of his love as its limit.

If the father's love is impure in this way, the question is to construct a love which can be guaranteed, continuous, faithful. There is surely the hint of such a construction at the start of *Mathilda*, where we learn of the father's completely devoted love for his wife: 'He loved her with passion and her tenderness had a charm for him that would not permit him to think of ought but her.' On her death, he mourns for the unusually extended time of sixteen years. And is not the father's suicide the ultimate act of love? 'You are the sole, the agonizing cause of all I suffer, of all I must suffer until I die,' he cries. Mathilda is now, like her mother, the one cause of her father's existence. We often speak in psychoanalysis of a woman's sacrifices for her father, but perhaps here we should focus instead on this fantasy of *the sacrifice of the father himself.* How can a father show the purity of his love if not by giving up . . . himself? Which means, once again, that the man becomes a dead man.

It would be an error, however, to assume that the weakness or the destitution of a father is contrary to the establishment of love. Mary loves her father for what he does not have. And indeed, a man may be rendered irresistible precisely at the moment when he is robbed of his manliness. Fenichel, one of Freud's followers, argued that in such a structure the woman comes to function as the instrument of which the man is deprived. When the man seems to be robbed of his masculinity, the woman comes to function as his phallus, the instrument without which he cannot exist: hence his surprising formula 'Girl = Phallus'. We see an illustration in the famous moment when Charlotte Brontë decides to choose the Reverend Nicholls as her husband. Having rejected his previous proposal, she listens to him deliver a sermon in church visibly shaken. Rather than speaking with the inner strength that would show him to be a real man, he delivers the sermon 'white, shaking, voiceless'. And now, it seems, her decision is made.

This shows that Brahms' rationalization of his failure to marry is a mere alibi: he claimed that he would not be able to face the questioning eyes of his wife after returning from the concert hall where he would no doubt fail to live up to his reputation. Everything proves, to the contrary, that such a display of weakness may be exactly what is required. To show one's weakness is to show one's lack, and is not love ultimately directed, as Lacan argued, to just such a lack, what he called castration. A man would thus be loved not for what he has but for his castration.

This is one conclusion suggested by the 'H.N. fiction' of Vita Sackville-West. The theme of weakness is a dominant one, as Vita encourages men around her to love her hopelessly, without committing herself. As Geoffrey Scott said of her, she was a woman who would 'ask for a possessive lover and do everything to show him he "possesses" nothing'. The man is thus put into the place of the one who lacks, a position which Violet was also trapped in. 'How gladly', she says, 'would I sacrifice *everything* for you . . . EVERYTHING.' Yet as with Scott, Vita could never become 'hers': she maintained the elusiveness which guaranteed the unsatisfied desire of her partners, while at the same time being assured that they, in contrast, *belonged* to her. This reminds us no doubt of her mother, a woman who systematically enticed the most wealthy men, *men who had everything*, in order to demonstrate that, in their love for her, *they had nothing*. The fact that the mother, Victoria, was everything for these men, indicated that they, in fact, were impoverished. To function as the object of the man's love thus implies that the man will be marked by a sign of weakness.

A clinical example gives a further illustration here. A young woman takes care to find partners who resemble her stepfather but whose wealth is always dwarfed by his own capital. Each time she speaks about her love relations, implicit comparisons with the stepfather emerge and she seems resolute, if not satisfied, to keep her partners suspended within this register. Hardly any material about her real father is forthcoming until a certain conjunction of events leads her to have the following dream: she returns home to find a girl in a white nightdress in her apartment. Her father is there carrying several shopping bags and he starts to speak to the girl in an animated way. This is followed by a second, shorter dream: the Eiffel Tower has fallen down in two pieces. Without going into the minutiae of the associations here, we must add one crucial detail, the fact that when she wakes up she is overwhelmed by a feeling of love for her father, something she claimed she had never felt consciously before. If the stepfather was a man skilled in the arts of speech and ostentatious in the display of his riches, the father was someone who prefered the frontier of his newspaper to conversation and maintained the most economic of lifestyles. So in the first dream he seems to be doing exactly what he does not do. Except for one detail: the bags from Galeries Lafayette are empty. The father is standing there with his hands full of shopping bags, but they contain nothing. All he is giving in the dream is his speech, and at that moment the daughter wakes up, with a feeling of love. On the side of the relations with men, she preserves a balance so that the partner always has less than the stepfather. This is the formula which keeps her desire going despite her inability to find,

97

as she said, 'something deeper' here. But the father, on the contrary, *is* loved, though not for what he possesses. He is loved precisely for his castration, for the fact that the bags from Galeries Lafayette are empty. If this daughter always took care to make her partners aware of the fact that her stepfather was, for them, nothing less than the Eiffel Tower, it is now the Eiffel Tower in pieces which is linked to the emergence of her sentiments. The key is the doubling involved, the fact that what is loved is loved *beyond* something else. If the stepfather's riches are loved beyond the boyfriends, it is the father's poverty which is loved beyond the stepfather.

Now, if a man's loving a woman constitutes him as lacking something and if to be an object of love may be so important for a woman, does this entail that her partner can never be anything but weak? It is interesting to note that when a woman meets a man sexually in an encounter of unprecedented sexual ecstasy, the relation is more than likely to be shortlived. A woman, speaking of problems in her relation with a man, evoked the indescribable pleasure of an affair she had had several years before with a photographer she had met in a chance encounter. She had never experienced such sexual satisfaction, neither before nor since. I asked her what happened to the relationship and she said that she had left the man abruptly. But, she added, she had no idea why. It had never been a question to her before and now that it had become a question, she had absolutely no answer. 'I just left,' she said.

If one inquires as to the reasons for the termination of such relations, it is rare to find responses. 'It just stopped' or 'I just left': but no more explanation of why. Paul Simon was clearly wrong: there are not fifty ways to leave one's lover. There are only two, the one that is explained and the one that is not explained. Perhaps this implies that a woman is not built to encounter The Man, or if so, as Lacan points out, it will be in the field of madness. Such relations of extreme ecstasy are notoriously shortlived. The Hollywood producers were wrong to make a film called $9\frac{1}{2}$ *Weeks*: if love usually doesn't last more than three years, relations of extreme ecstasy usually don't last more than two weeks. Men may well worry about being strong, but it is surely not for this that they will be loved. They are more likely to be loved for their worry than for their strength.

What about a man's love for a woman? Freud pointed out that a certain number of preconditions may be necessary. For example, that the woman be attached to another man, repeating the situation of the man's mother, someone who is attached to the father. Whether the man is aware of it or not, his choice will be conditioned by the presence of a number of small details, perhaps the colour of the woman's eyes, the timbre of her voice or something she is wearing. We recall the sequence of poems begun by the French man of letters Estienne Pasquier, taking as their point of departure the flea found one morning on the bosom of Catherine des Roches. It is as if the hymn to the woman's body is founded on something tiny, contingent. This little detail is crucial in the elaboration of love.

A woman complained that a friend had answered her question as to why he loved his wife with the response that he liked the way she buttered her toast in the morning. The questioner considered this an absurd and disappointing reply but in fact it is much more interesting and realistic

99

than the reply which evokes the radiant character of the partner. It is admirable as it gives key importance to a little detail, a stupid and senseless one. No matter if this man was aware of the fact that his wife's manner of buttering the toast was like his mother's: what matters is the stupidity of the detail since this is what love is all about.

In his commentary on the most famous text on love in the Western tradition, Plato's *Symposium*, Lacan gave a key importance to the figure of Agathon who is the focus of the protagonists' desires at the end of the text. The series of speeches of the diners is interrupted by the arrival of the drunken Alcibiades, who offers a sly encomium to Socrates in place of a conventional discourse on love. Socrates responds by indicating to him that despite what he appears to be saying, the real object of his lucubrations is in fact Agathon. Lacan stresses the stupidity of the young poet and the fact that after all the eloquent discourses on love, everything is reduced to this rather idiotic figure. Even if Lacan is slightly unfair to this prize-winning tragic poet, his point is a crucial one. It is also interesting to note that the dramatic genre of comedy, to which the *Symposium* belongs, so often treats of a man's ridiculous obsession with a single object, a box of money, a will and so forth, and the man in love is almost always rendered foolish and comical. In Congreve's *Love for Love*, the comedy of Ben's existence is the narrow horizon of the ocean: 'a man that is married', he says, 'is no more like another man than a galley slave is like one of us free sailors.' He is incapable of understanding anything outside the framework of his nautical concerns. Even when he is made to woo the distracted Miss Prue, his image of the 'voyage of matrimony' leads only to the prospect of swinging 'in a hammock together'. Everything is brought back to the same basic signification. Once the man approaches the woman, he is reduced, and rendered foolish, by this dominion of the detail.

One might object that foolishness there is simply because we are in the realm of comedy, but this response is clearly inadequate for a simple reason: *women, in comedies, are not reduced to idiots by love.* Meredith hinted at this in his essay on the comic spirit, by stressing the good sense maintained by the female characters. What comedy is showing us here is how man's love will ultimately focus on something senseless and foolish: like the buttering of the toast. A man in comedy is naturally a fool.

Details are certainly a precondition of a man's falling in love. But this is still not an adequate explanation. If it were, a man would fall in love with any woman incarnating the details in question. One cannot deny that this sometimes happens, but we need to look for some other factor to add to the presence of the various qualities linked to the woman's image. If the detail were the only thing that mattered all men would be fetishists. We would be drawn, as Pope said, 'by a single hair'. Sexual pleasure would be governed exclusively by the presence of a certain coloured ribbon on the woman's clothing. Or by the legendary shine on the nose. Freud had a patient who was drawn to women possessing this unusual attribute, and he traced it back to the homophony of the German word for 'shine' (Glanz) and the English word 'glance'. What the man wanted was to glance up a woman's skirts but this longing became inscribed in his life as the more reasonable, if singular, desire for a partner with the quality in question. Magazines are forever advising on what features a woman ought to have to become irresistible for a man, but the truth is both odder and more spectacular: the magnetism will depend on the unconscious constructions of the man, which can hardly be predicted. The partners of Freud's patient may have spent many gloomy hours wondering how any man could find them attractive given the luminosity of their noses. But their prince was out there somewhere. What could have prepared them for the man they were destined to encounter!

If all masculine desire has a component of fetishism at its horizon, if the little details are always necessary, something else must be added to transform an infatuation into love as such. A woman with green eyes must become *the* woman with green eyes. Cazotte offers us a number of clues in his fantastic eighteenth-century novel *The Devil in Love,* a text which Lacan encouraged his students to reflect on.

A young man, Alvaro, succeeds in conjuring up the Devil, who takes on a number of different forms. First of all, a hideous camel's head, then a spaniel and finally a beautiful woman, Biondetta. In this latter form, Satan binds himself to Alvaro, following him everywhere and acting the part of the lover. Alvaro does what appears to be his best to dismiss Biondetta and refuses to return her love. The beautiful image of this woman is not enough to capture his desire, showing us how love is not addressed simply to an ideal image. Something more must be added. The key episode occurs during a trip to Venice. Alvaro becomes the object of the attentions of a courtesan,

Olympia, who is immediately jealous of the mysterious Biondetta. Finally, she attacks her and wounds her mortally before the stunned gaze of Alvaro. And now the structure takes a new turn.

'What I saw now', Alvaro tells us, 'was a woman adored.' As he watches over her, he is convinced of her mortality and calls her for the first time by her name. 'Dear Biondetta,' she repeated, 'I am Don Alvaro's dear Biondetta.' Now, it is clear that Alvaro assumes the position of the lover from this moment onwards, so what has happened to change his relation with the image of the woman? The answer is simple: the image has been linked to a lack, it has been struck. In other words, it has become human. If infatuation is so often directed towards a flawless image, love is addressed to an image that has been wounded. If the Devil had first appeared in the form of a knowledge of things, able to provide Alvaro with whatever it was he requested and to ensure his success at the gaming tables of Venice, Alvaro's love is not directed to Satan as knowledge but to Satan as a lack of knowledge, a flaw in knowledge, as indicated in the reference to Biondetta's mortality. Love, as Lacan says, is ultimately addressed to a lack.

This conclusion raises a question. If a man's love is directed to a lack, how can we distinguish this from a woman's love? We have seen, after all, how the man's weakness or lack is essential for her. As a first response, we may say that love in general is directed to a lack. Where a woman's love distinguishes itself here is perhaps linked to the order of causality: the partner's lack must be guaranteed *by her*. Reverend Nicholls is white, shaking and voiceless because of her, Charlotte. She must function as the cause of the man's lack: her, rather than anybody else. A man, in contrast, does not always situate himself in this position when he is in love. Hence his demands for proof of the woman's love will be less frequent. Men do not always insist on being the cause of a woman's lack and when it appears to them that they might be taking on this function, they are likely to disappear. They panic and run off.

In fact, there is a fundamental tension here between the continuity of a woman's demand for love and the discontinuity which characterizes love for a man. It has long been observed how readily a man can fall in love with a different woman shortly after the end of a relationship. But this is far less easy for a woman. A man's love, even at an everyday level, is constantly subject to change, to oscillation from affectionate concern to wakeful suspicion and even hate. It is as if his ideal image of the partner is shadowed by the declamation 'Why aren't you someone else?' This implicit question, with all the hostility it brings with it, is picked up quickly by a woman.

Three forms of love may be distinguished here. Firstly, the mad form, the certainty that 'The other loves me' characteristic of paranoia. Second, the more female version: 'Does the other love me?' And third, the male version, 'Do I love the other?' While a woman may spend a great deal of time concerned about whether her partner really loves her or not, a man is more likely to spend his hours in doubting his own love for the one he has chosen. Hence one of the reasons for his swings between love and hate. But if the man's love thus changes, in a sense, from one moment to the next, perhaps a woman's love is something that preserves a continuity. A woman, from this perspective, may not fall out of love. Asked to define what love was for her, a woman replied, 'something which does not change from day to day'. But even if it does not change and love is directed to the same point, lack introduces itself in its own stubborn way. Loving the same person does not mean that you can't desire someone else. Or even several other people. If love is ultimately a demand, which aims to get rid of lack, desire shows its difference. It reintroduces precisely what love is designed to conceal, and hence the crises which emerge in love relations at exactly the moment when it seems that the partners are finally satisfied, that all obstacles to their love have at last been lifted. Something has to happen which will reinstate the dimension of lack.

This may be seen in a peculiar phenomenon. It happens from time to time that a woman has the urge to steal something. Let's assume that stealing implies creating a lack, making something missing, and hence is linked to desire. What is peculiar is not the urge to steal but the fact that often a woman experiences this at the moment that she has fallen in love, rather than at the moment that a love relation terminates. One explanation would appeal to the conception of theft as a way of getting back something that has been lost, but this would imply, contrary to experience, that the temptation to steal would emerge *after* a loss of love has been experienced. What one has lost in love one tries to get back via a theft. Focusing on desire, however, can make more sense of the emergence of the temptation at the beginning of a love relation: it is a way to keep desire going, to keep the lack in place, after the crystallization of love threatens to submerge it. It is a way to show, with great clarity, that demand and desire are not the same thing, that there is always something else which is missing, something that the presence of the real man cannot saturate. Let's see in more detail how demand and desire inform each other here.

Five

When Alvaro first conjures up the Devil, he appears in the form of a camel's head possessed, Cazotte specifies, of a remarkably large pair of ears. Now, what did the Wolf reply to Little Red Riding Hood's exclamation, 'What big ears you have!'? Answer: 'All the better to hear you with.' In other words, all the better *to hear what you are really saying*, what you are saying at the level of unconscious desire. Thus, for Little Red Riding Hood, we might hypothesize that what she really desired was to find a wolf in the bed. If we turn to Alvaro, we might pose a similar question. The Devil is at his service. So what does he ask for? First of all, a cold collation for him and his friends. Fruit, preserves, ice cream, Greek wine. Then a harp player. And at the close of this lavish evening of entertainment, Alvaro coolly dismisses what he had conjured up. But the Devil, in the form of the beautiful page Biondetta, does not go away. After the series of objects of his demand is exhausted, the bottles empty, the music mute, Alvaro is still left with something, perhaps the very something that the Devil's ears had allowed him to hear. When the Devil had asked '*Che vuoi?*', What do you want?, Alvaro had listed a number of objects, but beyond these objects of demand is the dimension of *desire*, what one wants at the level of the unconscious.

Comedy, once again, is alert to this dimension. When

someone demands something, they get something else in its place. When one of the twins in the *Comedy of Errors* asks for a sum of money, he gets a piece of rope. When a guest in *Fawlty Towers* asks for a Spanish omelette, he gets the pâté maison. In other words, one always gets something else. There is a fundamental incompatibility between what one asks for and what one wants. Children are alert to this when they play games like Chinese whispers. Sitting in a circle, a message is passed from one player to the next. When it has gone full circle, it has been dramatically distorted, showing how language is both what transmits a message and what necessarily deforms it. One could define desire as exactly this process: as the difference between the original message and that which arrives at the end. The key here is that desire is not the message itself. It is neither the original sentence nor the final one, but the process or structure of distortion itself. In Cazotte's tale, this dimension of desire is materialized in the form of the beautiful woman who will not go away, who binds herself to Alvaro and causes him innumerable problems. What he demanded was not what he desired, and what he desired was certainly not what he wanted or even needed. The Devil, to the extent that he heard Alvaro beyond what Alvaro intended to say, is in a position similar to that of a psychoanalyst. That's why he says to Alvaro, 'I had to deceive you in order to bring you to reason.' Manuel in *Fawlty Towers*, on the contrary, is not a psychoanalyst, because although his dramatic role turns on this principle of embodying the split between what one asks for and what one gets, the pâté maison which he provides in the place of an omelette is not linked to the specificity of the desire of the guest in question. He is less faithful than the Devil to the particularity of his victims.

Sensitivity to the difference between demand and desire here is prudential. If someone you are talking to continues to make slips of the tongue of a sexual kind, you might assume that their sexual desire is aroused. This may not be false. But men often conclude from the presence of such slips and other 'signs' that their companion, having their desire aroused, is interested in a sexual encounter with them. This mistake is at the source of so many fiascos. The key is to understand that demand is different from desire, that a slip of the tongue may testify to the presence of an unconscious desire, but this may be light years away from a 'conscious' demand. Desire, indeed, is there to persist as desire, not as anything else. It doesn't ask to be realized. Interpreting in the wrong way threatens this desire with extinction or collapse and so the other person will retreat to safeguard it. After all, maintaining one's desire is more important for most people than anything else, even friendship.

In clinical psychoanalysis, this fact is often ignored. Trying to explain everything to the patient will necessarily eclipse the presence of desire: if you supply a lot of knowledge, the dimension of lack is obliterated. What matters is preserving a place for what is between the lines, for what you don't know. If this place is maintained, it can function as a motor for the treatment and for the production of free associations. Get rid of it and the patient may well pack his bags. Helene Deutsch discusses a case in which the distinction between demand and desire is shown neatly. A man, fluent with the concepts of psychoanalysis, insists that, despite all this nonsense about transference and falling in love with one's analyst, he really does love her. He offers her theatre tickets and other gifts, and persists in his unlikely pursuit. None of Deutsch's interventions seem to have any effect until the moment when she turns to him and says 'OK, when do you want me to start divorce proceedings against my husband?' And of course, this does the trick. The poor man is disenchanted. To his continual demands, she replied with the possibility of a concrete realization, thus showing him that his demands were no more than the vehicle of a desire, something which did not aim at satisfaction. He wanted to demand, not to get what he demanded, in order to keep the dimension of desire in place. Deutsch's response offered him the collapse of his tactic, threatening as it did the real nature of his advances. Desire has to be maintained beyond the dimension of demand.

If Biondetta incarnates the residue beyond what Alvaro demands consciously, it is interesting to note that for the first half of the narrative Alvaro cannot name her. It is only once he has fallen in love with her that he can call her his 'dear Biondetta'. Up until this point, 'I could not pronounce that name.' The Devil is an 'x', an unknown quantity, something with no name, indicating exactly the nature of human desire, something which cannot be directly named or designated. Alvaro can name what he wants, the banquet, the Greek wine, the ice cream, but not what he desires. We notice, likewise, that just after the stabbing of Biondetta, Alvaro tells us that his state 'was indescribable. All other thoughts drained away.' There is a failure of words, of linguistic representation, and into this empty space comes his love for her and his ability to name her properly for the first time. The absence at the level of representation linked to desire is glossed over by love: it is given a sort of imaginary envelope.

Another example clarifies this idea. Calvino's character Enrico Gnei has just spent the night with a beautiful lady. That is all we know about it. No details of her appearance or of what they might have done, just the single sentence informing us of the encounter. As he passes the early hours of morning before going to work, he muses on the 'boundless Edens' his memory promised him if he could reconstruct the events of the night before. Bumping into an old schoolmate, Bardetta, he exchanges the usual appropriate conversation and then considers the effect of informing him of his recent encounter. 'The adventure of the previous night would have been able to leave a mark, take on a definitive meaning, instead of vanishing like sand in a sea of empty days, all alike.' By this time, however, his friend has left and Gnei is unable to catch up with him. He begins his day at the office and then, at a precise moment, is overwhelmed by a sudden, urgent love for the beautiful lady. The story ends with the image of an opaque whiteness wiping out 'every memory of sensations' and the anxiety of a man confronted with the impossibility of 'expressing, with hints or, still less, with explicit words, and perhaps not even with his thoughts' the fullness of the night before.

Where does Gnei's love emerge from here? It is linked to nothing less than the gradual disappearance of his memory of the encounter, the empty place where the representations of the adventure ought to be inscribed. We could say that his love is the sign of the fact that he can't remember. The theme of the story, after all, is the effort to transport an event into the field of signs, of representations, of memory. It is not that Gnei loves the woman and is trying to inscribe this original love in the register of memory or speech. On the contrary, the love is secondary: it *results* from the impossibility of registering the encounter. Love is the sign of a certain loss: it emerges in the place of a lack of a representation, just as we saw in the example from Cazotte. Note also that Gnei wants to catch up with Bardetta to tell him his story, as though his own memory is not good enough. What, indeed, is the function of memory if not to allow us to forget? Hence Gnei must try to register, to inscribe the events of the night not in his own memory, but in the memory of someone else. This is an interesting idea, the notion of having a memory outside oneself, of trying to make someone else act as one's memory. It shows, at one level, that our own memories are not there to remember with. That's why our memories are so incredibly large: there are so many things which we must forget as quickly as possible. We might then ask the question of why it is that women are much better at remembering birthdays and anniversaries than men?

Our two examples have shown us the way in which love is born from a certain gap. Calvino's character fails to elaborate this gap in any way which would avoid anxiety, but Alvaro, in Cazotte's tale, puts something very specific into this place. He puts the name of the loved one, Biondetta. Now, why should the name be so important here? And why is Biondetta so anxious that Alvaro name her? A name is, at the simplest level, a sign of recognition. Thus, Biondetta wants to be recognized, but the problem is that human beings spend their whole lives failing to recognize one another. In this sense, her demand is an exhorbitant one. A man in love may behave to his partner as he would behave to his mother or to his sister. Or he may desire a woman simply because she wears the same perfume as the woman he once loved. She is thus being recognized as someone else, not 'for herself'. All love relations involve this sort of misrecognition and this is perhaps the reason why elderly people go to the park to feed pigeons. In the wisdom that comes with age, they have realized that it is not by other human beings that they will be recognized. An animal will recognize you rather than mistaking you for someone else, as all pet owners know. Hence also the particular pleasure that adults experience when they think that their baby recognizes them: something, they know, which will not last for long.

In *Mathilda*, Mary Shelley gives this fantasy to her heroine:

My favourite vision was that when I grew up I would leave my aunt, whose coldness lulled my conscience, and disguised like a boy I would seek my father through the world. My imagination hung upon the scene of recognition; his miniature, which I should continually wear exposed on my breast, would be the means and I imagined the moment to my mind a thousand and a thousand times, perpetually varying the circumstances. Sometimes it would be in a desert; in a populous city; at a ball; we should perhaps meet in a vessel; and his first words continually were, 'My daughter, I love thee !' What ecstatic moments have I passed in these dreams!

The recognition thus involves a naming, 'My daughter', in fact, exactly the naming that Mary's real father shunned: after the elopement with Shelley and Godwin's subsequent reserve towards his daughter, she would wait beneath his study window in the hope of the sign that never came.

In the life of man and wife, perhaps the principal arena for the recognition of another human being is the argument. Civilization contains many debating societies but, as far as I know, no arguing societies, for the simple reason that arguing is what one does at home. What is more certain to arouse a woman's anger than the refusal of her partner to engage in an argument – or in other words, to recognize her? Men seem less bothered about this, perhaps due to their relation with their mummies. It shows how rather than considering an argument to be a break in the life of a couple, the period *between* arguments is the real interlude, the time when the couple fail to recognize each other on a daily basis.

Comedy, once again, is alert to these problems of recognition. What happens in the dramas of the fourth-century poet Menander and his contemporaries? A young man falls in love with a slave girl while his family pursue arrangements to conclude his marriage with the neighbour's daughter. But at the end of the play, it turns out that 'the slave girl' and 'the neighbour's daughter' are in fact the same person: there is a recognition that the two different descriptions in fact refer to the same object. The action had thus revolved around a continuous failure to recognize, and it is interesting that the ultimate object of recognition here is a woman. This is a key motif in the plays of Euripides, a poet who profoundly influenced the later comic tradition. We could contrast Electra's ability to recognize her brother Orestes with her more powerful inability to recognize her mother, Clytemnestra. She acknowledges her brother's identity via a scar, whereas her mother's exposure of her own breast to her daughter fails to make her recognized as the mother (in the sense of, a blood relation to be respected). Killing her, after all, implies that the mother is not recognized as the mother, and there is even a joke on this theme in the text. After the murder of Clytemnestra's husband, Electra becomes aware of some commotion and asks her brother, 'What is it? An armed force from Mycenae?' To which he replies, 'No, it's my mother.' The same motif is at the centre of the drama of Oedipus. He is someone who fails to recognize his mother Jocasta. Historically, there is thus a passage from failing to recognize a woman, in tragedy, who is one's mother, to failing to recognize a woman, in comedy, who is one's wife.

This comic thread is given elaborate development in another of Euripides' plays, the *Ion*. Creusa bears a child by Apollo, who grows up to become a guardian of the temple of this god, unknown to his mother, who assumes he died when abandoned as a baby. Creusa and her husband Xuthus now arrive at the temple in hope of some assurance of an end to the infertility of their marriage. Xuthus is told that his son will be the first person he sees on leaving the temple: and of course, this first person is Ion. So begins a series of comic misunderstandings, Xuthus assuming that Ion must be a real son fathered in a night of revel outside wedlock many years ago. Finally, a recognition scene takes place between mother and son by means of certain material tokens. Note that in all these examples, speech is an inadequate means of establishing someone's identity: recognition occurs only on the production of tokens, objects left with a child at birth and so forth. And note that once again the object of real recognition is the mother. In the later comic plays, the slave girl turns out to be an acceptable girl of good family, whereas in these plays of Euripides, turning-points between the tragic and the comic traditions, the woman's identity is somewhat more sinister. The mother always seems to be somewhere in the equation, but by the time of the comedies she has been replaced. The later comic poets chose not to conclude their plays with the equation: slave girl = neighbour's daughter = young man's mother.

If we interpret this replacement as a repression, comic drama finds itself with a secret history, and we see yet one more evidence of man's dexterity for anything except recognition. Another question emerges here: we have evoked the motif of the child's recognition of the mother, but what about the parent's recognition of the child? Psychoanalytic writers have often neglected this problem, preferring to focus on the relation of the child to its parents. We say that the child may function as an ideal or as a fantasy object for the parent, and although this is of course true it needs to be situated in the appropriate context: that of the relation of the parents with the grandparents. In other words, the fact that a mother might expect the love from her son that her own father failed to give her. We remember the Freudian thesis that a woman's wish for a child is an extension of her desire to be given a child by the father. Now, given the presence of love in this relation, there is nevertheless a certain hatred, linked to the father's original refusal of love: after all, he failed to give her something. Thus the child becomes the site of both love and hate, an ambivalence which we see in the labour pains that sometimes appear long before confinement or in the excessive anxiety of certain mothers that their baby might fall. Phyllis Greenacre noted the related phenomenon that after the collapse of a marriage or love relation, the rawness of a mother's attitude to her children may become apparent, a rawness which she characterized as sliding between spiteful possessiveness and revengeful abandonment.

The troubled relation of mother to child is often so strong that a woman may dread the possibility, during pregnancy, that her baby will be invalid or deformed. Indeed, it is a fact that some women choose not even to become pregnant due to a morbid certainty of this outcome. Prospective mothers spend more time telling their friends of their fears ('It will be a monster', 'It won't survive') than in articulating their hopes and dreams about the child's future. This is the flip-side of the idealization of the child: the more the image of the child is ideal, so the negative ideal is set into place, just as hate functions as the subtle or not so subtle shadow of love. On becoming pregnant, the question may arise to torment the mother, 'I've waited so long for a child, how can I really have one now?', or, 'How can I have a child who will not be ill?' The more the promised baby becomes imminent, the more the original disappointment in love from the father is made present. This disappointment is inscribed onto the very image of the child to be born.

No mother–child relation can escape the presence of some measure of unconscious negativity. Even in the simplest case of a mother's longing for a child, what happens to this longing after its birth? If the *idea* of the child had been linked up until then with the idea of it not being there, once it is there, the longing or the desire must find new pathways. Perhaps this explains the various food cravings a mother might experience during pregnancy: once the baby is there, inside her, the motif of there not being something becomes linked to all the little objects (chocolate, shrimps) which were important in her own relations with her mother. Important not for what they were, but as signs linked to whether the latter would reply to her demands or not. In this relation of asking and demand, the object itself (the chocolate, the shrimps) is abolished as such, becoming merely a sign indexing the love relation to the mother. Decades later, it can emerge in the pregnancy craving since it is being loosened from the main current of desire focused on the baby itself. Alternatively, cravings might be explained even more simply: now that the woman's libido is centered on one image, that of the baby, other fixation points are disinvested, hence coming closer to consciousness. They are discarded and fall away: hence the weakening of the cravings in question after the baby is born. These explanations are interesting, but it is also probable that they simply embody the mother's cannibalistic fantasies towards the child: 'little objects' are the focus of the cravings because the baby is, after all, a little object. Such hypotheses are more likely than those which evoke an instinctual appeal for vitamins and iron.

Children pick up on all this quickly. If the idea of lack is linked to the baby and then the baby emerges, it can understand perfectly well that there is something in the mother's behaviour and speech which *still* makes its presence bound to an absence: hence the child itself may try to fall, to vanish or to incarnate 'not being there' in some way. The image of the vanished or stolen baby exerts an extraordinary fascination in our culture, when the real prospect is generally unlikely. It serves to represent, in the privileged space of the media, this unconscious current in psychic life which always returns to the motif: the baby isn't there.

Psychology betrays its own unconscious involvement in this structure with the famous 'visual cliff' experiment. Originally rationalized as a way in which to study early human perceptions of depth, a table top is covered with a transparent medium which goes beyond the visible edges of the table itself. In the first version of the experiment, baby goats were placed on the table and then confronted with the appearance of their mother some distance away. More goats chose not to 'go over the edge' than to attempt the perilous passage to the mother, but with human infants this was not the case. Several of the babies persuaded to take part in the experiment went over the visual cliff and into the (imaginary) abyss. Now, rather than claiming that this shows how *babies* are alert to the dimension of lack, that they are in fact trying to fall, a thesis which is neither demonstrated nor unlikely in this context, why not see the significance in the very invention of the experiment itself?

It shows the laboratory construction of an apparatus which links the idea of the presence of the mother and the disappearing child, the child who goes over the cliff, who vanishes for the mother. It is an example in which it is worthwhile paying attention to what Lacan called 'the desire of the experimenter'.

For the father, things are also complex. He might expect from his daughter the love which he did not receive from his mother. This would explain the hostility of many fathers to their daughter's first boyfriend: his presence reminds the father, in the most tangible way, of the fact that his own mother's love was not faithful to him. There was another man around: his own father. The effects of the boyfriend's arrival should thus not be underestimated, just as, for the mother, the girlfriends of her son will be subject to the most uncalled for critiques. Any fortune teller who wishes to remain in business is well aware of this: she will take care not to make optimistic pronouncements about the perfections of the son's future bride. And as Helene Deutsch once said, a mother will endure promiscuity in her son much more readily than his monogamous love for a woman.

A man sees his thirteen-year-old daughter kissing a boy in the bar of their hotel. The next day, father and daughter go shark fishing. The boat develops engine trouble and a terrific storm descends on the flimsy vessel. The crew panic but even now, with the prospect of imminent destruction, father refuses to say so much as a word to daughter. The slight, the slap to the father in the kissing scene, is thus more powerful than the question of life or death. The father's unconscious attachments pay no heed to the urgency of situation: they remain untouched. What the daughter did is genuinely unforgiveable, evoking as it does the profound infidelity of love.

If Biondetta demands recognition and finally receives it when Alvaro falls in love, what sort of recognition is really at play? It is hardly worthy of that which comes from the pigeons since it is still based on a misunderstanding or, indeed, a deception. Alvaro finally recognizes Biondetta as Biondetta, but, of course, this beautiful image is the Devil himself. It is only at the moment that Alvaro says to her 'You alone suffice: you fulfil all my heart's desires,' that she abandons her name for the first time: 'Biondetta must not suffice. That is not my name. You gave it to me.' In other words, Biondetta is the name of your fantasy. The beautiful image dissolves and Alvaro now sees before him a hideous camel's head surrounded by huge snails. Biondetta no longer exists, showing Alvaro that she was merely the embodiment of his own desire: when this desire evaporates, so does the phantom image. Only when she finally 'sufficed' and thus when the dimension of desire collapses does she reveal what she really is. In a sense, it is the moment when the Devil really does become a woman, the moment when she says to him 'You don't know me.' Or, as we suggested earlier, a psychoanalyst. The Devil does not require a pound of flesh here. What he wants is far worse: the truth. He aims to show Alvaro how the object of his desire is nothing less than the form of that desire itself, how love is constructed out of a lack, exactly like the analytic transference which may be given the very formula used by the Devil here: 'I had to deceive you in order to bring you to reason.' It is only through the experience of love that you can understand something about the illusions it is based on and the abyss it is there to conceal, which is why the Devil does the only ethically correct thing possible once Alvaro is truly captivated. He reveals himself for what he is.

Whereas behind the image of Euripides' Helen there is nothing, behind the image of Biondetta there is something, something unsettling and all too present. It is the point of horror around which Alvaro's desire has been organized, the element which his dream of love had done its best to put to sleep. At the end of the book, he is led to question the reality of many of the adventures that have befallen him, but the real question is the reality of desire. We remember the common device, used in literature and cinema, of the man who dreams, for example, that he is in a desert, has many adventures and is then abruptly woken up by his alarm clock. As he gets up, looking fondly back on the dream, he finds a grain of sand in the bedclothes. In other words, the reality at play in the dream is somehow more powerful than the reality to which he awakes. The desires operative in the unconscious are what structure our waking reality, even if we are completely unaware of them. Like the buttering of the toast, the grain of sand is the little detail which indexes the register of desire.

Six

Is to receive a love letter to be recognized? If the field of love is structured by misrecognitions and misunderstandings, can the simple and direct expression of a love letter succeed in going beyond them? And if a woman's sexuality does not speak to a man, is there not a contradiction in the very idea of a love letter? Is this why women in love write more letters than they post? Remember the scene in *Love in the Afternoon* of Audrey Hepburn burning her letter to Frank Flanagan or Kim Novak destroying the letter she has just written to James Stewart in *Vertigo* revealing her true identity. Does it suggest that love in fact actively prevents the transmission of a letter? This might explain why when lovers do send their letters, they so often make a mistake with the address: 12 rue de Tournon instead of 2.

We could start by contrasting the letter as a message and the letter as an object. In Middleton's *The Widow*, a married woman receives a love letter. She shows it, outraged, to her husband, who then makes it known to the author that he is aware of what's going on. But in fact, the woman had written the letter to herself. By showing it to her husband, she proves her own good intentions, and via the husband's response to the other man, she sends him the message of her own bad intentions. This is a well-crafted schema, one which we find also in a tale of Boccaccio. The letter here is sending a message at several levels, but although its consequences may be sexual, there is no eroticization of the document itself. What matters is the signification, the meaning, of the letter.

Valentine Dale had the same idea. This diplomat from the court of Elizabeth I needed cash, so he wrote to his Queen detailing his financial position, enclosing with the same packet an affectionate letter to his wife which included reference to the monetary difficulty. The letter to the Queen was addressed to his wife and vice versa, so that Elizabeth was both surprised and amused to find herself reading a text replete with 'sweetheart' and 'dear love'. Touched, she sent the cash to her Valentine, unsuspecting that the 'blunder' had been carefully and deliberately engineered by the diplomat. The vignette shows that Rodin was wrong to identify his famous statue of the headless man with a diplomat: someone who, lacking a head, does not think. The canny ambassador was both flexible and fertile in intrigue, appealing to the letter as signification, as the purveyor of a message.

Joyce's famous Trieste letters are in striking contrast to such a transmission of information. He writes obscene prose to his wife Nora, suggesting that she do unspeakable things with the actual letters themselves, such as inserting them into the orifices of her body. The letter here is less a vehicle of meaning than an object as such. Sewing one into the lining of one's garment, as was once common, has the same effect: it matters for what it is and where it is rather than for what it says. Like Lady Caroline Lamb's letter to Byron, which was made up of the precious fabric of her pubic hair. There are thus at least two functions of a letter: as a message and as an object. Does this tell us anything about the different relations a man and a woman may have to letters sent and unsent? Would a letter remain unsent if it functioned as an object and become sent if it were the vehicle of a message?

This answer is too simple. After all, a letter may sometimes function as both message and object. We might turn to the register of industry for a clue, but again the criterion doesn't seem to be the right one. If women write more letters than they post, does this mean that they write more letters anyway? Madame de Sévigné's endless letters to her daughter or Emily Dickinson's continuum of poetic fragments find their reflections in the field of male writing. If a Juvenal could write less than four thousand lines in a period of thirty years, a Petrarch could not go anywhere without his writing materials being within easy reach. If quantity does not constitute a compass here, perhaps the *relation* to quantity does. We are all familiar with long literary descriptions and perhaps we might put forward the hypothesis that one of the functions of male writing, in contrast to that of a woman, is to send the reader to sleep. This is quite serious. It evokes a sort of generalized version of Caryl's project to write a commentary on Job: running to more than 1,200 folio pages, its design was to inculcate the very virtue of patience of which the commentary treated. Or, the early novels of the French author Robbe-Grillet, where a simple household object may be detailed for page upon page. The ways of art, of course, are various, but one suspects that such activity aims at mortifying not simply the object described but also the readers. People sometimes speak of a written work as a monument, something to commemorate the life of the author, a tomb. But since a characteristic of many tombs is to remain empty, it becomes clear that a text may be written with the real intention of becoming equally abandoned: to become a volume deserted by every reader. And just as a tomb aims at an addressee situated beyond its explorer, many of those writers who mortify themselves in their activity have no other addressee than that which lies beyond their mortified readers: death. Perhaps Voltaire had understood this, if it is indeed true that he dictated part of his *Henriade* to his secretary while asleep. Schoolkids are sensitive to this factor when they ask their parents why the writer they are studying used up ten pages to describe a house instead of one. To answer this with the reply that the longer the description, the clearer the image of the abode, is clearly unacceptable: witness the fact that no one agrees on what exactly Pliny's villa looked like although it is lovingly described for page upon page.

Such attempts at mortifying the other are well known in psychoanalysis. Lacan pointed out the way in which many obsessional patients speak continuously, even supplying interpretations of their own material, in order to block the analyst from saying anything. This sort of dialogue with oneself reminds one of Cato's effort in the Roman Senate to prevent the key moment of a vote by discoursing for as long as possible. After all, wasn't it the right of a senator to speak on any subject for as long as he wished before a motion was put to the house? And likewise, is it not the patient's right to say anything that comes into his head? Such tactics have the effect of putting the analyst in the place of a corpse, someone who might as well not be there. One of Lacan's patients wrote of his scandalous treatment by the psychoanalyst: while he was in the midst of his 'free associations', Lacan left the room to take a phone call or to get a cup of tea, remarking as he left the office, 'Don't hesitate to continue the session during my absence.' Rather than seeing this with the patient as a gross breach of professional dignity, we can understand it as a response, an interpretation, to precisely the sort of situation we have been discussing: the patient speaks so as to put the analyst to sleep, to maintain him in the place of a corpse. Lacan's unusual manoeuvre had the effect of countering this by sending the message back to the patient that he might as well not be there.

Although there are female obsessional neurotics, this sort of speech relation is rarer in women. It is interesting that there are many books about women and writing and a woman's sexualization of the creative process, but very little is said in psychoanalytic literature about the relation of a woman to speech. Why is this? In a certain patriarchal tradition, a little girl must keep silent: it is for the boy to speak. We could evoke the image of Charlotte Brontë's timidity and tonguetiedness when she met the writer Thackeray at a London dinner. But if this is the case, surely stuttering would be more common among girls than among boys?

If to stutter is to experience a difficulty in entering the world of speech, wouldn't the place assigned to the girl in the family structure entail that she would be the one to flounder? But, as all speech therapists know, this is far from the case. Boy stutterers are far more common, and various half-baked explanations have been given as to the girl's agility at avoiding this problem. One way of understanding the phenomenon of stammering would be to link it to the boy's passage through the Oedipal structure and the problem of situating himself in relation to his father, the moment of assuming the mantle of speech. Speech would belong to the field of what one *has*, and hence any difficulty in assuming it would be indicative of a reticence to grasp something which belongs, symbolically, to someone else, to the father. Boys frequently admit their discomfort with the image of going on stage in front of their class or school, that is, going into a place where they have to assume something. This shows that what matters is not the message, the dimension of what one is saying, but rather the place of speaking itself. The key here is to distinguish speaking and being called upon to speak. Stammering is not a difficulty in speaking but a difficulty *in assuming a place from which to speak,* a position in a symbolic network. We could say that in fact stammering is not the only barrier into the world of speech. There is another alternative, which functions as the mirror image of stammering, even though it is not treated as a speech disorder: ventriloquism. This is another way, after all, of not having something. It is the other who speaks, not the subject. We could say that stammering and ventriloquism constitute the two thresholds of the speaking world, both indicating a troubled relation to one's symbolic place there.

It is no accident that professional illusionists, people who are interested in producing fictive images for the mother, of pretending to supply her with the image she is searching for, so often relate their early interest in ventriloquism. Failing to enter the Oedipal register of having, it is a question rather of being, of being something for the mother. An example from the psychoanalytic literature illustrates this problem of having and not having for a man. A young man plagued with the most serious of stutters contracts a venereal disease and, rather than chastising him, his family show delight and, for the first time ever, the father walks him arm in arm to the movies. From this moment on, the stammer disappears. Why? In terms of the Oedipal model, it is because the young man has finally really lost something: the venereal disease evokes the presence of castration. The father now treats him as a man, in other words, as someone whose having is based on a not-having. He couldn't speak because to speak meant to be called to his place as a man. It is no accident, then, that he reports a dream that he is visiting a prostitute after a 'very fine gentleman' had just left her. He is fixed to the spot and can move neither limb nor tongue. His presence in the dream is thus that of someone who is always preceded by another man, a man from a different register, as is indicated by his fineness: this is no doubt the paternal register. And this shadow is what blocks him from moving forward, it is what paralyses him completely. The speech trouble is thus rooted in the problem of transmission from father to son, from stepping into the place of the very fine gentleman. It is exactly the difficulty of a Dr Johnson, a man who refused on one famous occasion to step into his father's place in a bookstall. That this problem in situating symbolically the relation of father to son was posed through the register of speech for Dr Johnson is clear from the isolated narrative of his dream. Out of the paucity of dream material of this acerbic and brilliant speaker, there is the one recorded image involving a vicious contest between two orators, which he lost.

If this perspective on stammering explains its frequency among boys, it is still not enough to account for the lack of female stammerers or, indeed, for their occasional presence. Remember the children's games we evoked earlier: if a little boy wants an object currently possessed by another child, he may well use force to snatch it away. But a little girl is more likely to appeal to someone else. Whereas what matters for the boy may be possessing the object as such, for the girl what matters may be the desire of the other party. There is a sensitivity to the desire of the other, and since this desire is routed through speech, perhaps the female escape from the stutter makes more sense. The desire of the other is engaged with more dexterity than for the boy. His problem is less productive: he wants the object possessed by the other child and to get it entails the destruction of this rival. But to destroy the rival would be to destroy one's own desire, since the only reason the object is valued in the first place is due to the fact that it belongs to someone else. This always determines the passage of the tea trolley on British Rail: whereas female travellers frequently request a refreshment when the trolley is passing, men tend to wait until the person in front of them has ordered something before deciding that they too require refreshment. The object becomes necessary only once the other person has shown their interest, in exactly the same way that a man may ignore a female colleague for years at work until the day when someone else shows his interest in her: then it's unrequited love. This structure should not be confused with its female version: if a woman is more sensitive to the desire of the other, that doesn't mean she'll want to *possess* the same object. Rather than ordering the refreshment on the train, she might decide to deprive herself of it, and thus to maintain her desire. The man's rush to possess what he assumes is an object of desire only generates the impossible: if you possess too quickly, you've got rid of desire.

Hence the boy's desire is in an impossible situation: to get what he wants would mean no longer wanting. This is one of the reasons why men spend most of their lives oscillating between the love and hate of their friends and partners: they have to maintain their rivals in order to preserve their desire and yet they have to destroy them at the same time. They have to have a boss in order to desire the boss's wife, but to desire the boss's wife implies destroying the boss. Anyone who has been close to a man understands this. It's why when men make slips of the tongue, so much hostility is at play. Where they make slips like 'You disappear', a woman is more likely to say something like 'I disappear', in other words, 'I want to let the desire of the Other speak through me, to make my desire the desire of the Other.'

This also gives us a clue to another curiosity: if a boy is paralysed at the level of the syllable, many women complain of not being able to finish not words but *sentences*. Men often take advantage of this to finish their sentences for them, but to do that is to miss the point. Not to finish a sentence may often indicate a hesitancy to be pinned down by words, to show that one is not equivalent or identical with a particular linguistic representation, to be something more than what one says. Men and women know that their existence cannot be reduced to words, but men do their best precisely to reduce it to this: hence the many rituals they may introduce into their lives. The dimension of 'life' is literally extinguished by the tyranny of their habits or the verbal formulae which can return to torment them in obsessional neurosis. A woman, on the contrary, may make it the most urgent of tasks to show that this absorption of everything into language can never be achieved: that there is a gap between language and existence, that one cannot be reduced to a word, a description or a meaning. Now, to finish a sentence pins down its meaning. The writers of the seventeenth century exploited this feature of language, new clauses continuously functioning to change the sense of the preceding ones. Leaving one's sentences, and perhaps, one's letters, unfinished may thus indicate a refusal to be made identical with a meaning. We saw earlier on how a current of female sexuality was concerned with questions of meaning, and we may link this with the motif of the unfinished. If a man's absence is made to mean something, a woman's presence may sometimes aim at not being identical with one particular meaning. The letter is not posted for the simple reason that it remains eternally unfinished.

A woman writes a letter to a man she loves. She carries it around with her for several weeks, and each time she reflects on it she decides to rewrite it since so many new things have happened, so much in her life has been changing. The letter continues to hibernate: there is never a right time to post it, since whenever the 'right time' is reached, time has passed and there is more to write. The letter may not be posted, as we just said, for the simple reason that it remains unfinished, but this simple reason suggests another one: the letter is unfinished because *the person who wrote it is unfinished.* As new things happen, she is continually becoming distinct from what she had originally described. Her life is always a little bit ahead of the description, and perhaps the respect for this gap is dearer to a woman than to a man – who, as we saw, aims to make the gap vanish, to absorb his changing life in language. Men and women are both unfinished, but by posting his letter a man may aim to obscure this; a woman's unposted letter, on the contrary, highlights the unfinished nature of the sender.

Not finishing may also indicate an appeal to the desire of the Other, something that becomes clear in moments of prayer. As one nun says, 'I understand prayer to be a state of mind in which one allows God to be God and doesn't constantly interrupt, saying "Here I am."' In other words, 'I leave myself and my ego out, and become aware of God's activity.' Prayer would thus be 'the activity of God within one': one speaks but it is the Other who is speaking. The subject vanishes and the question of the prayer becomes identical with its response: speaking to God is no different for this nun from God's activity itself. Both prayer and song may characterize one aspect of a woman's relation to the Other to which she addresses herself, something which cannot be touched and which is maintained, precisely via prayer or song, in the dimension of the beyond. The difference between men and women here is simple: if a woman often wants to be *a part of* God, a man, on the contrary, frequently wants nothing less than to be a God. This shows the different relation to what is beyond one. If one's addressee is not tangible in this way, what sense would it make to post a letter?

This question of the addressee introduces the problem of the perspective point, crucial for the study of men and women. Listening to a traveller praising the orange groves of Genoa, Stendhal thinks of being able to share their coolness with his lady, *with her*. The firework display in the *Elective Affinities* must go ahead even if all the other spectators have left: as Eduard says, they are for Ottilie alone. It is the addressee who becomes crucial, the perspective point from which the lover's focus is assured. Such modes of presence are often more explicit for a woman. Looking at herself in a mirror, she may say 'Doesn't Jennifer look good today.' In other words, the spectator is manifestly a component of the subject's own view of herself. And even if she doesn't want to, a woman is often quite aware of the fact that she is behaving exactly like her mother, an awareness that often produces an acute feeling of self-hatred. This function is much more repressed with men. A man who drives a fast car in a reckless way might well be putting on a display for his father, even if the latter is nowhere in sight. He is incorporated into the subject's relation with himself, but the driver will not be particularly alert to this. Hence the difficulty in the analysis of many male subjects of indicating to them the place of this third party who is the real addressee of their actions. That is why a man's neurosis is like a map: to understand what is going on, you need to find out from where the perspective is fixed.

The idea of the perspective point is a crucial one. If you want your daughter to be discouraged from her identification with Madonna, it's no good telling her that she doesn't look like Madonna or that she can't sing in the same way. The key is to find the perspective point, that is, less the question of with whom she is identifying than that of *for whom* she is identifying. Perhaps during a domestic quarrel she notices that her father's eyes keep straying to the television screen where Madonna is performing. There is a difference between the image you assume and the problem of who you assume it for. When Boswell wrote himself a memo 'Be like Johnson!', he might have paused to ask himself who he wanted to be like Johnson for.

This distinction can offer a new perspective as to how Shakespeare's shrew got tamed. The standard interpretation is that Katharina stops acting like a shrew after Petruchio shows her the folly of her ways by behaving badly himself. He makes her realize what it is like to live with someone whose conduct is unbearable and she is brought to reason. But this is like saying that the girl will renounce her identification with Madonna if you show her a mirror, which is false. Petruchio's strategy is, after all, nothing but a cure by mirrors as he supposedly shows her what she is like. The key, then, must be situated elsewhere, in the register of the point of perspective.

The first question to ask is, For whom does Katharina assume the image of the shrew? It is clear that she misbehaves the most when the gaze of her father is close at hand. Thus prior to the question of curing her of her shrewishness, one has to situate her identification in relation to its addressee. And she has every reason to be a shrew for him: it is the father, after all, who decrees that the other sister Bianca can only be married once Katharina has been married off herself. This is a raw deal. Katharina is supposed to accept her position as, literally, an object of exchange. She refuses this and becomes, as a message to the father, a shrew. But if the Madonna identification cannot be undermined by pointing out real discrepancies between teenager and star, how are we to explain the taming of the title?

An identification can only be modified by affecting the place itself of the perspective point. If Katharina is a shrew for the father, this implies that any taming will be less a consequence of Petruchio's antics than a change in the status of the father. This is exactly what happens in the play: Katharina's metamorphosis follows the scene in which the figure of the father is unmasked. A pedant made to impersonate Bianca's lover's father confronts the real father, and all the imaginary attributes of paternity are put in question. Thus, the problem of what it means to be a father is posed in all its disturbing clarity. And it is only now that Petruchio and Katharina can kiss . . . It is by having an effect not on the relation of someone to the image they assume but rather on the point from which they are looked at that change can be introduced.

If the taming is made possible by affecting the perspective point, what does it actually consist of? It is nothing less than a linguistic torsion, a modified position in relation to language. Katharina starts the play by refusing to be an object of exchange. When she opens her mouth, it is not so words can be substituted for each other, but so that words can hit people. Hence the bite of her tongue and her appeal to material objects with which to thump people. Words for Katharina are there to strike their objects. But what has happened by the end of the play? Words now are not made to strike but to be exchanged: in the famous taming scene, she accepts the interchangeability of the words 'sun' and 'moon' regardless of the situation of the sky. She will call the sun the moon and the moon the sun. She has thus moved from a classical to a contemporary theory of language. Words no longer have a direct relation to their objects but form part of a network of differences. The word does not have an intrinsic relation to its referent but may find a substitute in another term. This linguistic turn is exactly what is introduced and made possible by the paternal unmasking that precedes it.

How does this emphasis on the perspective point help us to understand the problem of the letter? It seems to be addressed to one person, and yet it can only be understood with reference to the place from which it is being read by someone else. When Madame de Sévigné says that she doesn't like writing except if it is writing for her daughter, we may still assume the presence of a third party. It is the crucial question of *Whom for?* When Charlotte Brontë sent off the manuscript of the first book of poems by her and her sisters, she informed the publishers that there would be no need to return the original manuscript together with the page proofs: they would be able to do the corrections with just the proofs as they had the poems by heart. If letters and poems are remembered for someone else, we could ask the question, Who had the Brontës remembered their poems for? They had no flesh and blood sweethearts at the time. What were the poems aimed at? We have seen that the addressee of a letter may be distinguished from the perspective point, the place from which the writing is surveyed, what Milton called his 'stern taskmaster'. And often it is true that a love letter just does not aim at the real person it is sent to. What matters is who reads it, not who it is sent to. When Stanley Spencer continued his correspondance with Hilda for nine years after her death, the physical existence of the addressee was clearly not required. The letter functions here as an index of the void left by the loss of something precious. It would thus not be addressed to a woman, but to an empty place which the woman is made to occupy. We saw in the stories by Calvino and Cazotte how the man's love is constructed out of an empty space which is marked by a lack of words or signs. The production of love letters would thus be a way of elaborating this space, of framing an emptiness.

Madame de Sévigné's correspondence with her daughter illustrates this attempt to put something, a letter, in an empty space. When the daughter leaves her mother to live with her new husband, de Sévigné writes more letters in the eighteen months after the separation than in her first forty-five years. 'My letter', she says, 'is infinite, like the love I have for you,' a sentiment which is embodied in the physical form of the letters themselves, many of them running to more than twenty pages of her enormous scrawl. From the moment of separation, she tried, for twenty-five years, to find new ways of saying how she loved her daughter. The letter is infinite because this cannot be said, a fact which was both the torment and the test of her existence. She describes the agony of separation as 'that thing . . . susceptible to no comparison', and thus as something which cannot be represented in language, the characteristic of which is precisely to permit analogies and substitutions of words. The chain of letters aims to demarcate and to fill, in a certain way, the void left by the absence of the partner. As all her contemporaries noted, when her daughter left, she was transformed into a changed creature: her correspondence is the authentic diary of a lover.

A woman's love letter, if such a thing exists, does not, of course, have to follow this particular logic. It does not have to aim at filling out a void or an empty space. Rather, it may have precisely the function of *making* a void, of literally creating a hole. Let us take the example of Emily Dickinson. She characterized her poetry, in a famous phrase, as her 'letter to the world', and yet what does this letter do if not, via its elliptical grammar, make a hole in the world?

Soft as the massacre of Suns
By Evening's Sabres slain

This letter confronts us with a dazzling opacity of reference. What is 'soft as the massacre of suns'? The poem does not fill in a void, it creates one, the void of the subject of the poem itself. As the critic Cristanne Miller has pointed out, the compressed and disjunctive grammar of Dickinson's poetry makes almost every poem into a sort of abyss. And if we take her identification of her poems with letters seriously, it ceases to be evident whether a letter ought to have a meaning. One might write precisely in order not to mean something.

The problem is that for the man, the meaning of a love letter is so important. On receiving a love letter from a woman, he may strive to understand it, to read into it, to find metaphors and hidden references. But there is no reason to suppose that the letter means anything. A man will try to put meaning into this empty space: to try to make the woman's body speak. But a woman's body will not, ultimately, speak *to him,* even in love. If a man's love letter speaks, but not necessarily to the woman he loves, a woman's love letter does not have to speak, in this sense, at all. When the man receives a letter that says 'The window of my bedroom is banging although there's no wind outside,' he'll spend ages trying to work out what it is saying. Is the reference to the bedroom an invitation? Is the banging window the same as the beating heart? Does the fact that there is no wind outside mean that the force is coming from the inside? But the letter might not mean any of this. All it might mean is that when the writer sat down to write, that was what was going on around her. The only thing for sure is that her letter is more of a love letter than anything which says 'I love you.' Maybe that is what a woman's love ultimately involves: the possibility of sacrificing meaning, of not having to mean anything. The problem, as we've seen, is that what a man's love ultimately involves is exactly the opposite: the resolute search for meaning and the refusal to let anything not mean something.

Language, unfortunately, works against this. Meanings are not so easy to pin down. Even the most personal intention, the most intimate message, the feeling closest to your heart, cannot be transmitted without problems. To say 'I love you' is the most difficult thing in this sense, as it has at least three canonical and disparate meanings:

a) I'm tired.

b) I want to engage in coitus.

c) I'm having an affair.

But of course, it can mean something else.

So why not post a letter? If its relation to meaning may vary, this would not seem to affect its delivery, yet it is certain that many letters remain unposted. A letter which stays at home may be a letter which is unfinished and it may also be a letter to oneself. Violet writes to Vita, 'I love in you something which is not you but me.' A part of 'ourselves' may remain, as she implies, outside us. Lacan elaborated on St Augustine's notion of that which is 'closer to us than we are to ourselves', the idea that we search for a part of ourselves that has somehow been lost outside us. In this sense, the limits of the body are not the limits of our biology. A part of us is somewhere else. Thus, the meaning of *writing to oneself* changes.

To reformulate the problem, we find a clue in an odd phrase of Lacan's. A woman's love, he says, aims at the 'universal man'. Now, by definition, this will be situated beyond the real male partner. How, then, can one send something to him, and is it even necessary that he *knows* that something is being sent? If Freud's considerations on the condition of forbiddenness are taken seriously, it is not certain that the love object should even be aware of his value. The continuity of love is preserved so long as the latter does not reply. There is thus less risk of a perturbation and the misunderstandings which are both constitutive and disruptive of a lover's dream. After all, if he knows, he'll try to understand and to extract meaning from the letter. It is written to someone beyond the real man, yet it uses him as a relay, in exactly the way that a real man may be used in a sexual relation as a relay for a woman to get somewhere else, to a different space. In their first moment of real physical proximity, Daphnis and Chloe are bathing in a grotto. Chloe touches Daphnis' body and then immediately moves her hand to touch herself. Her relation to herself, to her own body, follows a circuit which includes but goes beyond the body of the man. If the man is still around when this circuit is completed, he may complain of his exclusion and his alienation from the woman's enjoyment. He is no longer necessary.

Space seems to be the important concept here. It is clear that a woman's body extends beyond its biological limits in a way different from that of a man: witness the difficulty with which women move house in contrast to the relative facility for the man. Men are able to live in conditions of extreme disorder, often to the utter consternation of the opposite sex. This is interesting. Does it not disprove the popular notion that women are more narcissistic than men? Men can live in squalor because all their narcissism has been focused on themselves, on their own ego: hence they can be oblivious to the state of their apartment. This may be tested empirically: see if the most narcissistic men tend to have the most untidy apartments. In contrast, women are so often minutely attentive to the details of their space, indicating that if narcissism there be, it is of a different nature to that of the man. It is more spread out, encompassing the body and the surrounding space. As Reik pointed out, the space is less the substitute of the body than the *continuation* of it. This importance of the living space has its effects on the sexual relations of men and women. Indeed, it is perfectly possible for a woman to decide not to make love with a man once she has seen his apartment, whereas the reverse situation of a man changing his mind for this same reason is rather unlikely.

The more focused quality of male narcissism is seen clearly in the relative speed with which men will become involved with a new partner shortly after the end of a love relation. In a sense, they can do this because their unconscious narcissistic link to the mother is so strong – the unconscious position of being the satisfying, darling object for the mother – that what actually happens from one female partner to another is diminished in consequence. The link to the mother may be so deeply entrenched that hardly anything in the real relation with the partner can touch it. Perhaps the reason a woman's narcissism is often more elastic, more spread out, as we said, is due to an initial difficulty in investing the ego as such: hence it will divide itself between the body and its image and the surrounding space. The limits of the body itself become enlarged.

The fact that a woman might store her letters with her clothes rather than with her files and books might be related to this thesis: they are closer to the body. This is not enough, however, to explain the proximity to the wardrobe. Another condition has to be added: the fact that a letter incarnates the dimension of that which has been *given*. Anything which evokes this register is going to be put in a relation with the body (stored near clothes) since what the body tries to envelop is what can be given, particularly from a man. When Lady Caroline Lamb decided to burn Byron's letters to her in her outrage, she had to burn special copies of them instead of the originals. What had been given by the dangerous poet was still cherished beyond her immediate suffering since it incarnated the dimension of what he gave.

The childhood memories of a woman converge on one scene: it is Christmas and a humpty-dumpty waits at the foot of her bed. Her mother tells her it is the father's gift and she runs to his bedroom to thank him. As he wakes up, she sees from his bewildered expression that he had no knowledge of what he was supposed to have given her. So many years later, she remembers this scene and her feeling of joy despite her realization that the toy had no doubt been chosen by the mother. What mattered was the fact that, in her words, he accepted, at that moment, 'the role of the one who gave'. There is thus a separation between the real father and his function or role: he was allocated the role of giver, and this dissolved the particular bitterness that might have followed from the discovery of his ignorance as to the choice of gift. The childhood memory thus shows the priority of the function of giving over the specificity of what is given.

Giving for the man is different. The more a man gives the more he aims at the destruction of his object. To give, after all, is a demand. Divorced couples know this: some husbands insist on giving so much to their exes as a way of remaining in touch or, more precisely, of suffocating them even more with their demand. It's simply not true that husbands always want to keep all their belongings to themselves. The irony is that the more generous they are, the more selfish their love is, with only obliteration at its horizon. In the same way, a woman is right to be suspicious if a man showers her with presents. The more a man gives in the register of material goods, the less he has to give at the symbolic level: the more presents he bestows, the less he can give at the level of the phallus, the more desperate his love is. This may be tested empirically. The troubled relation to the assumption of masculinity will so often have this effect: the man gives too much. Which might even take the form of premature ejaculation. Perhaps this is not unrelated to the fact that he may end up posting more letters than he should. He may lack the internal limit which will guarantee that some things are not given. Contrary to a popular misconception, men often want to give *everything*. That's why they are so bad at keeping secrets from their wives.

And even the simplest gift has its malignancy. What reason can there be for a man to give a woman perfume out of the blue? There are only two possibilities: it is the same perfume used by his previous love or he is captivated by an advertisment which manages to strike a chord with his unconscious fantasy. And in both cases, he does it out of the blue because he is guilty about something. This is why civilization maintains the festivals of the birthday and of Christmas. They are occasions sanctioned by society when we are supposed to give presents and we don't have to show our guilt. Neither a birthday nor Christmas come out of the blue. But take a moment to think about why the man brings you flowers today rather than any other day and they may start to wilt.

It is a fact worthy of attention that in the work of many of Freud's early followers, guilt was seen as a central, perhaps *the* central, problem of psychoanalysis, and yet today it is more or less neglected. Why did this happen? Does it mean that we have already understood what guilt is all about or rather that guilt is just not a particularly important concept? In everyday life, it is without doubt a ubiquitous sentiment. Many people feel guilty simply when they walk past a policeman. The Freudian explanation here supposes that even if we have not carried out a real crime, our unconscious desire is enough to generate guilt feelings when we are confronted with someone or something which represents the law. We are guilty in thought, not in deed. This argument led some of Freud's students to the belief that real crime is often carried out precisely in order to pin down this guilt as a sort of alibi: 'Look, I've committed a crime, this is what I am guilty of, not anything else.' We thus break the law to escape from the responsibility for our unconscious desire. Although there is certainly some truth in this perspective, things can't be quite so simple: witness the fact that at the airport many people have a momentary feeling of *satisfaction* when the bleeper bleeps going through the security check when they *know* that they are not carrying anything in the nature of contraband, and yet walking past a policeman they do not have the same feeling of satisfaction. This indicates a more subtle relation between innocence and guilt.

A conman, the 'Duke', dreams up a magnificent plan. He installs himself in a smallish town in the States and opens an account at the local bank. Various minor transactions go through. Then on the Friday night he goes to the car showroom, points to the most expensive sportscar and says he'll buy it immediately, with a cheque. Now, in a town like this one, sports cars don't get sold every day. The customer is saying, furthermore, that he'll take it as it is, no changes, added accessories or modifications. In other words, it is the sale of a lifetime for the showroom employee. But, there's the question of his cheque . . . it's too late to call the bank and it's a Friday. The salesman trembles and hesitates. And then he takes the cheque. Now, what does the Duke do next? He takes the car and drives it to a used car dealer close by and asks to sell it, for cash, immediately. It's a small town, the dealer makes a couple of phone calls, the police arrive and the Duke is arrested. And then, on Monday morning, the cheque clears. The Duke sues the police for false arrest and negotiates compensation with the dealer. It really is the perfect scam to crown the achievements of a professional.

But what exactly is the Duke's plan about? There is first of all the problem of what he is stealing and then the question of the production of guilt. He engineers a situation in which all the signs designate him as a conman. The immediate resale of the car is the obvious indication that the cheque will bounce. Everything points to a criminal action. And yet the Duke is showing that he can escape from the significations generated by this context in which anyone else would be a thief. He is relying, after all, on social conventions and codes to make the plan work: in this system, someone who buys a new car with a cheque and sells it five minutes later is up to something. We could say that he is cheating less the police or the car dealership than language itself, as embodied in the codes and conventions of society. He is cheating a code and thereby displaying his *difference*: he has the right, after all, to sell the new car to whoever he pleases. The idea is that if social codes, conventions and language are what deprive us of our difference – since if we act in a certain way, that will imply a particular significa-tion – the Duke is claiming his difference back: this is the real object of his theft. He is showing that he can slip away from the meanings normally generated by a particular set of actions. He is thus trying to cheat the grandest opponent that exists, the symbolic order that makes the whole plan possible in the first place. What he is trying to cheat is language itself.

Now, what does this tell us about the relation of inno-cence to guilt? The lesson is a logical one: it is precisely by his innocence that the Duke is truly guilty. Although the whole scenario is designed to generate for the car dealers and the police the signification 'conman', it is only by being innocent, by having signed a valid cheque, that he really does become a 'conman'. He becomes this at the very moment that the police and car dealers recognize him as innocent. If it seems as if the Duke's innocence is what makes him guilty, we can still be more precise. Two senses of 'guilty' should be distinguished here: the standard social meaning and the deeper psychoanalytic one. The Duke would be determined as guilty by society only on condition that he *included himself* in his 'innocence' from the start, if he gave himself a place within the whole scenario as it was originally conceived. The problem, however, with the Duke is that, being a conman, his job is precisely not to include himself in things, not to be responsible for what he says or, on other occasions, for the cheques he signs. His son became a writer, and so took the opposite path. In signing his name to his work, he assumed the mantle of responsibility for what he said and wrote, and accepted that he would ultimately be judged by the effects of signification which this work generated.

This introduces the second sense of the term 'guilty'. Being guilty now consists in something very simple: not taking responsibility for what one says. The more the Duke tries to slip away, the more he is constituted as guilty. The key is that he *fails* to include himself in his own scenario from the start, and this failure to include oneself is identical with what guilt consists of. Thus analysis can have an effect on feelings of guilt, for example by making someone work through their own inclusion in some unconscious scenario. The child who helplessly watches the parents making love must ask himself why he stayed at the bedroom door for so long, or what unconscious identification or assumption he made at that moment. It is a question of realizing that one's innocence becomes identical with one's guilt the moment one really assumes it. This is, as Hegel saw, the basic structure of the story of Oedipus.

The Freudian argument has another implication here as well. One way of theorizing guilt is to see it as the gap between the ego and the ideal, the point which you always aim at and always fall short of. Psychic life, from this perspective, involves a striving towards some ideal. If, by some unhappy chance, this ideal is attained, the most terrible forms of depression may ensue. The worker who is suddenly transformed into the boss or the athlete who breaks a record will have a significant price to pay for their closing the distance with the ideal point. This is the key difference between the advertising campaign for the various pools companies and the National Lottery. The pools companies present images of someone enjoying the fruits of wealth, but the Lottery reduces its advertising formula to the simple phrase 'It could be you'. The pools thus assert the implicit proposition 'It could be your neighbour', the other man who is living in luxury. It is an advertising campaign which appeals, in part, to envy. But the minimalist formula of the Lottery does something different. It does away with images, reducing its effect to a pure linguistic phrase (plus pointing finger), one which, furthermore, has a sinister echo. 'It could be you' reminds us of the other huge advertising awareness campaign of the 1980s about HIV, with its own implicit and explicit message 'It could be you'. There is certainly something very menacing about the National Lottery campaign (which ensures its success), something which involves an appeal to our guilt. 'It could be you' is a perfect example of a superego imperative. It is like an order, a command. We buy the tickets to pay back the agency represented by the Lottery for our sins, thus making the Lottery as such exist. As Sextus Empiricus said a long time ago, the gods must exist because if they didn't we couldn't serve them. We have to pay a price for our own existence and in paying it, we construct and feed the very body that demands something. This guilt factor means that there is no such thing as winning the Lottery since to play, one must have already lost. Winners win only in their daydreams and if, by some terrible chance, they win in reality, the problems really start.

And the alternative? Preserving the distance between you and the ideal point only generates the guilt of not getting to where you ought to be. You are reminded of this distance by the superego which holds the ideal up to you as a mocking testimony of your failure. Now, what is going to happen to this picture if we introduce the presence of a love relation? According to one Freudian model, the loved object will take the place of the ideal: one will behave to this person as if they were exempt from criticism and truly ideal. The consequence, however, is that if the loved object is put into the place of ideal and guilt is a relation between ego and ideal, being in love will generate a profound feeling of guilt. This argument, in a somewhat more complicated form, was modified by Freud's students Jekels and Bergler many years ago. They claimed that love in fact releases one from guilt as it deprives the superego of a means of demonstrating to you that there is a gap between the ego and the ideal: if the loved object also loves you back and overestimates you, the ideal can no longer be used to remind you of your inadequacy. Thus, they claim, the enthusiasm and ecstasy of a lover comes less from any link to the real love object than from the brilliant idea of cheating the superego.

This sort of argument may be tested by asking the question: Have you ever loved anyone who did not make you feel guilty? If the answer is negative, the fact that gift-giving is so common in love relations will become easier to understand. And also, perhaps, the fact that men sometimes post more letters than they ought, dispatches which they afterwards regret. When Lord Monmouth sent secret missives to France written in lemon juice and was subsequently discovered, his guilt is demonstrated in this refusal to find a more prudential form of secrecy.

A man who had been married for many years showed that this guilt had a very particular condition. Whenever he sat down at table with his wife and turned to the plate in front of him, he was immediately overwhelmed with a feeling of having perpetrated a crime. When he ate alone, this never occurred. At one level, the guilt was linked to the presence of a traditional lover's triangle: the husband was divided between his love for his wife and his real passion, which was focused on the oral object. The true object of his libidinal life was linked to the plate of food, something equally reflected in the choice of sexual technique adopted with his partner. Such a preference might seem rather far-fetched but it is common knowledge in psychoanalysis. The real question which one might ask here is rather, why was it necessary for this man to get married at all, given the nature of his priorities?

This is exactly the question posed by a young woman, in love and engaged, who takes her fiancé home to a dinner with her parents. Before the latter have sat down at table, the fiancé starts to serve himself from an enormous bowl of stew. And the young woman knows at once that this is not the man she will marry. She breaks the engagment almost instantly. We have discussed already the importance of the detail in love life, but here it is less the detail which fixes or generates the sentiment than the sign which closes it. This gesture of the fiancé was all it took to disclose the priority for him of his oral drive, showing the woman the abyss between the field of love and the field of sexuality. It is exactly this tension which is discussed by the psychoanalyst Ludwig Eidelberg in an amazingly eccentric investigation of slips of the tongue. A man goes into a restaurant with his date and asks the head waiter for a room for two. Now, one might well imagine that he meant to ask for a table but because what he really had in mind was a sexual adventure with his date, the stronger motive declared itself: a room instead of a table please. Eidelberg refuses to be fooled. He thinks that the slip shows that what the man was desperately trying to avoid was the focus on his orality, and that the slip, the reference to the room, was a sort of alibi to throw his conscience off the track. What he really wanted was a big table of food. Thus, the whole theory of slips of the tongue is put in question. When you make a lapsus, is the 'new' word that emerges the repressed element itself or, on the contrary, is it that the 'intended' word, the one which did not emerge, is the real clue to the repressed complex?

Given this implicit tension between the key place of the oral drive (or indeed, any other) and the partner, what on earth can a couple do? Was the young woman right to abandon her fiancé so swiftly? Should the guilty husband always have to go through an ordeal when he eats in the presence of his wife? We have highlighted many negative things about the relations between the sexes in this book. Some readers might even find its outlook pessimistic. The only solution to the question 'How do men and women live together?' would seem to be: they get jobs. But now here's something positive, a recipe, no less, for more successful relations between partners. Freud, we remember, had recommended an acceptance of the idea of incest with parent or sibling. Why not add to this the following modest condition: to live the priority of the drive with some humour. The scenes we have described in the last paragraphs are not without a comic aspect. Perhaps this aspect would emerge with more clarity once it is accepted that although drives may be tempered in some ways, they have both a singularity and a selfishness which can never be eliminated.

We have seen throughout our discussion how the gift has a very different place in the fields of masculine and feminine sexuality. The importance of form, of the container, which we evoked on the female side can give us a clue to several related questions. For example, why is it relatively rare to find female pyromaniacs? Why is it boys who play with matches? The classical psychoanalytic explanation for pyromania links matches and fire with the phallus, but this would imply that girls ought to be equally interested. Perhaps the answer involves a shift in perspective: if, for the boy, what matters are the matches and the flames, perhaps for the girl the key variable is not the agent of fire but its *object*. A girl expressed her revulsion towards flames with the remark that the burnt object might contain babies. In other words, what mattered to her was not the flames which would engulf the house, but rather the house itself and what was inside. Small girls often situate their imaginary babies not in their tummies but 'at home' or in a dolls' house, as if the house were the first envelope of the infant. The house is too close to the body, and to the baby, to get burnt. There is thus a sensitivity to the relation of form to content, to jewel boxes as well as jewels. Envelopes have real value, something rare in little boys. How many men, indeed, keep the wrapping paper from their presents?

This relation to form also serves to explain why women

are rarely claustrophobic, contrary to popular mythology. The 'disaster movie' shows us time and time again a group of people trapped in a small space. Time is running out and some of the assembled party become hysterical: in general, the women. But this is strictly a cinematic fiction: in such situations, it is invariably the *men* who become claustrophobic. Department store owners are well aware of this fact. Women are perfectly happy to browse through labyrinthine displays for hours on end whereas men need space. Thus men's sections are often housed on the ground floor of the department store in conditions of relative openness. A more authentic Hollywood project would be to film the drama of the team of male warriors waiting inside the Trojan Horse. And if the inhabitants of Troy were exclusively female, the Greek team would probably not have had to worry about the risk of fire.

It is amazing how popular conceptions of female panic fail to register these differences. The object of panic is so often distinct here. Women who go scuba diving may well be terrified of the occurrence of a particular underwater situation or the arrival of an unfriendly fish but male divers repeat again and again the same formulation of their unease: it is not that they fear a specific situation or fish but that they fear being afraid. They panic about the very possibility of getting into a panic, in other words, about losing their self-control, about disappearing as masters of themselves. Indeed, as we saw in earlier chapters, while a woman may organize her fantasy life so as to stress her own disappearing, a man does his best to avoid precisely this disappearance: it is the one thing he must devote his whole life to guarding against. To use Lacan's analogy, he constructs for himself an immense fortress to protect against this. The price to be paid is the tedium and discomfort of living in a town under siege. The better the defences, the worse this will be. He will always be imagining what this fortification looks like *from the outside*, without recognizing what it means to be living on the inside. Perhaps this explains why a man might spend all his free time in gardening or attending to the front of the house yet be completely oblivious to anything that needs doing inside it.

These examples show ways in which the relation of men and women to form is fundamentally different. For a woman it may be something involving both inside and outside. But for a man it involves, more often than not, one side only: and what he does with this is to bang his head against it. If a woman uses her antennae to pick up desires around her, a man uses his to get stuck in other people's antennae. It is unlikely that he will understand that it is an insult when one woman says to another 'I always admire you in that dress.' Or that it is sometimes best not to do the same thing as someone else. Look at all the problems caused by the conflict of Richelieu and Buckingham over the Cardinal's refusal to insert a line change between his 'Sir' and the start of his letter as decorum required. Buckingham's reply, which repeated the gesture, shows two men locked in the battle of forms. They were only capable of doing the same thing as the other. Richelieu's manservant was canny enough to grasp the nature of this dynamic. When the Cardinal engaged him in a favourite pastime, a jumping competition to see who could reach the highest point on the wall, the manservant took care not to win.

All this should not be taken in the apologetic sense. Men, it's true, often glorify the 'antennae' of women, but only in order to avoid confronting something else: as a way of articulating the unconscious assumption that if they, the men, don't have something, the woman does. This can create neuroses and also traffic problems. Some male drivers assume that they don't need to use their indicators since female drivers will somehow just guess what they are going to do. Or, in love relations, that the woman ought to give them something, even if they themselves can never be exactly sure about what this *something* is.

The sensitivity of women to the desires around them in this domain does not need to be a mystery. To respond to the glorification of the so-called 'mystery' of femininity, one may evoke a little detail about childhood. Whose reactions can we generally predict? The mother. And whose reactions will be basically unpredictable, whose fondness or anger can rarely be forecast in advance, the one who will represent the real mystery for both sexes? The father. Who knows when he's going to lose his temper? We could say that when a woman seems mysterious, the mystery has a very precise formula, that of the question: How much can she live without a man and how much does she depend on one? The balance between these positions is an infinitely delicate one. Indeed, we could say that, for a man, this balance just *is* what is so often called the mystery of women. Men either adore this – a defence – or they are terrified. But it is a fact that those men who spend their lives professing their terror or contempt of women always end up getting married, whereas those who continually discourse on their love of the opposite sex are quite likely to end up single.

What is interesting here is that admitting to being afraid of a woman is so much more humiliating for a man than admitting to being her slave. Hence the badge of subjection assumed by many men, a way of indicating the false knowledge that one knows what one's partner wants. In other words, every time she says anything which could be construed as expressing a concrete desire or want, the man jumps, so eager is he to be able to give a name to the desire of his wife. But his wife, on the contrary, may not be so keen. Perhaps her letters will remain unposted. And perhaps men keep love letters with their files and other letters for the simple reason that *they are letters*. Women don't because for them these objects are not always letters. A letter can be a letter or it can be something else. If it is something else, it doesn't need to be posted. What matters is that *one wrote it* and perhaps it was written to no one but oneself. This reverses the wisdom that we converse with the absent by letters and with ourselves by diaries and it shows us how writing, perhaps, is ultimately not meant to be read. When the *Iliad* of Homer was transcribed within the space of a nutshell and the Bible in that of an English walnut, the scribe had really understood something of what writing is about.

The letters of Audrey Hepburn in *Love in the Afternoon* and Kim Novak in *Vertigo* remain unread and unsent. The first was intended to warn the playboy Frank Flanagan of the imminent attempt on his life, the second to reveal to James Stewart the fact that the woman he has just met, Judy, is in fact one and the same as the woman he believes dead and whom he loves so much. But both women chose not to send their letters. And they both did the same thing instead: they put themselves in its place. Audrey Hepburn shows up at the Ritz in Flanagan's suite, and Kim Novak decides to see if she can make Stewart love her for what she really is, not simply as the copy of another woman. If a letter is there to name you, to describe you and to represent you, and if words can never say everything, a letter will always remain unfinished. Both women, aware that writing wasn't enough, put themselves in the place of the letters they did not send. Which raises the question, if not posting a letter can be a sign of love, is receiving one the sign that love is undone?